Modelling Fallschirmjäger Figures

Jaume Ortiz Forns & Daniel Alfonsea Romero

Consultant editor Robert Oehler • *Series editors* Marcus Cowper and Nikolai Bogdanovic

First published in Great Britain in 2006 by Osprey Publishing
Midland House, West Way, Botley, Oxford OX2 0PH, UK
443 Park Avenue South, New York, NY 10016, USA
Email: info@ospreypublishing.com

ISBN-10: 1 84176 896 0
ISBN-13: 978 1 84176 896 0

Page layout by Servis Filmsetting Ltd, Manchester, UK
Index by Alison Worthington
Originated by United Graphics Pte Ltd, Singapore
Printed and bound in China by Bookbuilders

06 07 08 09 10   10 9 8 7 6 5 4 3 2 1

A CIP catalogue record for this book is available from the British Library.

FOR A CATALOGUE OF ALL BOOKS PUBLISHED BY OSPREY MILITARY
AND AVIATION PLEASE CONTACT:

NORTH AMERICA
Osprey Direct, c/o Random House Distribution Center, 400 Hahn Road, Westminster,
MD 21157, USA
E-mail: info@ospreydirect.com

ALL OTHER REGIONS
Osprey Direct UK, P.O. Box 140 Wellingborough, Northants, NN8 2FA, UK
E-mail: info@ospreydirect.co.uk

www.ospreypublishing.com

Photographic credits

The photographs that appear in this work were taken by the
authors.

Acknowledgements

The authors would like to express their thanks to Carles Elias,
Oriol Quin, José A. Azorín (Stug), Pedro F. Ramírez and Taesung
Harms for their help, which was invaluable in the successful
completion of this work.

Dedication

This book is dedicated to the women in our lives – Teresa, Laura,
Emma and Diana, who have certainly deserved it, for their
enduring patience and boundless support.

Contents

Introduction

The coveted paratrooper qualification badge.

From its early beginnings as a battalion in 1936, Germany's paratrooper branch grew to a body comprising several divisions. About 230,000 men served as Fallschirmjäger throughout the Third Reich period, the greater part of them during World War II, when paratrooper units were engaged in every major campaign, earning an elite status, admiration and respect even from their enemies.

This image seems to have endured in our own hobby area, and Fallschirmjäger are plentiful in the figure market, making this popular subject an excellent choice for this series of how-to modelling guides.

Of the diverse subjects dealt with in this book, painting techniques take the lion's share; given the limitations of space, we reasoned that it would be natural to prioritize this, the most widely followed discipline. We hope that the many modellers who concentrate on painting out-of-the-box figures, as well as those who also indulge in figure conversion, will both profit from some of the techniques explained in the painting tutorials. We have also found that painting techniques are especially well suited for a step-by-step presentation. Our chosen medium is acrylic paint, which has steadily gained popularity in our hobby.

We have also dedicated some space to converting and scratchbuilding figures, hopefully encouraging the modeller to try to expand his horizons, and use a commercial product not as an end in itself, but as a basis to accomplish an out of the ordinary, more original project.

We have tried to present a balanced choice of subjects; accordingly, the most popular sizes (1/35, 54mm, 1/16) and materials (plastic, metal, resin) in which World War II figures are available have been included.

We engage in our hobby from a historical modeller's point of view, and try to do detailed research before beginning projects, to ensure accuracy. We understand historical miniatures should have both accuracy and artistic appeal. This is just our personal choice, and every modeller should feel free to choose their own framework, but we genuinely feel research widens the possibilities and results in more satisfying models.

Each chapter is prefaced by some brief historical notes, to put each subject in context, and some basic explanation of Fallschirmjäger-specific uniform development and details. This is not meant to be more than an introductory guide, and we invite you to consult the bibliography at the back of this book for fuller details of such topics.

This book is the product of joint authorship; we have worked as a closely knit team, developing the initial idea, designing the individual projects, researching the subjects, and bringing them to fruition. The only differentiated tasks were figure conversion and scratchbuilding work, carried out by Daniel; and the all-important painting and final presentation job, the responsibility of Jaume, because these happen to be our particular areas of specialization. We did so believing that this combination of efforts would, hopefully, result in a more complete and better result: the book you have in your hands. Now it is up to you to judge if this is indeed so!

As a concluding note, we the authors would like to remark that our intention throughout this work is to encourage the reader to pursue new challenges in the hobby. If we have managed to entice you to do a little more research when planning your next modelling project, or to try to paint that camouflage pattern you find so daunting, or to dare to undertake some conversion work, or to attempt for the first time a vignette or diorama – then we have fulfilled our objectives.

OPPOSITE Fallschirmjäger figures involved in Operation *Merkur*, Crete, May 1941, in an illustration from Osprey Publishing's Men-at-Arms 139 *German Airborne Troops*.

'Ready to jump': early Fallschirmjäger, Operation *Merkur*, May 1941

Subject:	*Fallschirmjäger in early uniform and jump equipment, Operation* Merkur, *May 1941*
Project overview:	*General techniques with acrylic paints, solid colours and face painting. Tips on creative groundwork.*
Modellers:	*Jaume Ortiz and Daniel Alfonsea*
Skill level:	*Intermediate*
Base figure:	*Verlinden Super Scale 120mm (no. 1228)*
Scale:	*1/16 (120mm)*
Additional materials used:	*Tamiya 'Surface Primer' (no. 7026); Tamiya X-21 Flat Base.*
Paints:	*Vallejo Model Colour: Matt Black 950, Brown Sand 876, Basic Skintone 815, Burnt Cadmium Red 814, Luftwaffe Blue 816, Dark Sea Blue 898, Chocolate Brown 872, Olive Grey 888, Grey Green 866, Sunny Skintone 845, Orange Brown 981, Khaki Grey 880, Offwhite 820, Light Grey 990, Desert Yellow 977 Iraqi Sand 819, German Camo Black Brown 822, Leather Brown 871*

Introduction

German paratroopers earned their elite reputation during the blitzkrieg era. In 1940 they took part in several major campaigns in the West, including Norway, Denmark and Belgium, undertaking actions such as the capture of the Belgian fort of Eben Emael. In 1941 the Fallschirmjäger (FJ) fought in Greece and featured prominently in Operation *Merkur*, the assault on the island of Crete. Compared to earlier actions, this was a massive undertaking, comprising four FJ regiments plus additional FJ Corps units, launched by parachute and glider, together with airlanding and seaborne mountain troops.

Although ultimately successful, the high number of casualties suffered in the Cretan campaign meant that it would be the swan song of large-scale airborne operations.

This chapter is dedicated to general techniques with acrylic paints, with an emphasis on the very important area of face painting. A large-scale 120mm resin figure, a Verlinden Productions item, provides an excellent medium through which to showcase a basic tutorial. This project portrays an archetypical early-war paratrooper, and includes parachute equipment. Some tips on creative groundwork, as a means to enhance single figure presentation, are included.

Our soldier is kitted out with the well-known specialized equipment developed for paratroopers: his jump smock is a step-in, second-model example; these existed in several minor variations of pocket configuration. It replaced the first-model jump smock, which was used only in pre-war times. Known as the 'bone sack', this garment was mainly manufactured in a grey-green mixed (*grünmeliert*) cloth;

OPPOSITE The finished Fallschirmjäger figure.

incidentally, the origin of the 'green devils' sobriquet applied to the German paratroopers by the Allied troops lay in this clothing (although a transitional model in splinter camouflage pattern saw limited use, coexisting with the third-model smocks). The 'bone sack' is worn with the field-grey (*feldgrau*) jump trousers (note that these were never manufactured in field-blue cloth), easily recognizable by their side pockets; and with the early side-lacing paratrooper boots. For safety, he has donned a pair of padded knee protectors, and, of course, the characteristic M38 helmet. His parachute is the RZ 16 type.

Other than a pistol, German Fallschirmjäger carried no other equipment on themselves when jumping; the rest of the items and weapons were dropped separately in containers, which had to be recovered as soon as possible in the landing zone, not a particularly efficient arrangement, especially when the containers went astray and the enemy was in the vicinity. It is not surprising that paratroopers improvised ways of carrying more substantial firepower on their persons. One such container will be built as a fitting complement for the figure.

The scene is set in an airfield: the paratrooper is making final adjustments prior to climbing aboard the Junkers 52 transport plane for the drop on Crete. If you look closely, you may notice there is more than one 'green devil' ready for the jump …

Painting with acrylics

In this chapter, our aim is to introduce acrylic painting techniques. With this in mind, we will develop two step-by-step tutorials, one for faces and another for unpatterned clothing. The choice of a large-scale figure will help in this, and has been purposely selected.

Acrylic painting is based on a simple principle: the superimposition of transparent layers of paint, thus creating a blending effect between two contiguous hues. Transparency is achieved by diluting paint with water. The more water you mix in, the more transparency you get.

Normally, the base colour is applied in two or three moderately thinned layers, to ensure that no surface detail remains uncovered. Next, you prepare the highlight tones, adding to the base colour small amounts of the colour selected for the effect. These highlights will lighten the base colour, and will represent those areas more exposed to light. The number of highlight applications will depend on the position of a given volume with respect to the source of light, and on the degree of contrast you want. Next, you similarly prepare shadow tones. Again, the number of applications and their intensity will determine the final contrast.

In our figures, we always try to apply the concept of zenithal lighting; that is, we apply highlights and shadows as if the subject was exposed to a source of light placed directly overhead. In my opinion, the results are much more attractive than with the 'general' lighting method; zenithal lighting gives much sharper contrast, which brings a scale figure to life.

Large-scale figures, as in the present case, demand softer contrast than small-scale figures; you must look for a compromise between realism and contrast effects, to avoid your figure becoming a caricature – and the larger the figure, the more careful you must be.

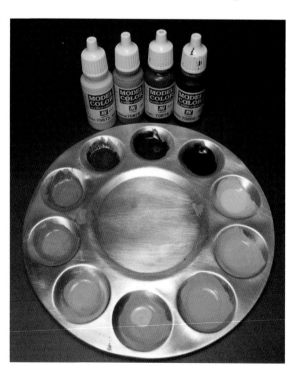

The palette with each paint mix ready. You can see there is a gradual colour scale, from lightest to darkest.

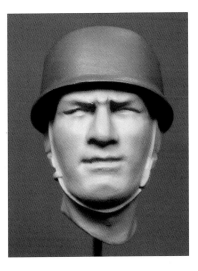

The face, primed with Tamiya's Surface Primer. I favour light grey priming, because every detail is clearly seen.

The base colour, Brown Sand 876, applied in two thin layers, thoroughly covers the face.

The first highlight. I add Basic Skintone 815 to the base colour, and lay it over the most prominent areas.

Nevertheless, such advice should not be taken as dogma: sometimes, you will want to apply less contrast to particular areas. Coherence in the final result is the most important thing.

We have used Vallejo acrylic paints throughout the book, a personal preference, but these technical concepts are equally applicable to any other brand.

Painting faces

First you must prime the figure. It will reveal any imperfection in the surface, either from the casting process or from our preparation and assembly stages; these flaws may be easily missed, and are more difficult to correct at a later stage, when you have begun to paint. Also, obviously, primer doubles as an undercoat, giving a smooth surface onto which acrylics will set properly. I use Tamiya's Surface Primer, in grey.

Next, prepare the highlight and shadow tones. I recommend a ten-well aluminium palette (see the photo on page 8). Any impermeable container would do, but I find this kind of palette especially useful, because it allows me to have all the tones I am going to use readily to hand: the base colour, four highlight and four shadow tones, and black.

For the base colour, I use Brown Sand 876; Basic Skintone 815 is mixed into it for the highlights, and Burnt Cadmium Red 814 is mixed in for the shadows. The first highlight has 25 per cent of Basic Skintone, the second 50 per cent, the third 75 per cent, and the last is 100 per cent Basic Skintone. The first shadow has 33 per cent of Burnt Cadmium Red, the second 66 per cent, the third is 100 per cent Burnt Cadmium Red, and the fourth is made with this same colour mixed with 20 per cent black.

These colours are mixed by eye. You must obtain a perceptibly gradual colour scale progressing from the lightest highlight to the darkest shadow, in the palette.

Most painters apply up to ten progressive highlights and as many shadows; this is because they try to achieve the blending effect from the very first layer. I prefer a technique similar to that of working with oils, 'blocking' the extreme shadows and highlights at the beginning, and then blending them with glazes.

The basic, highlight and shadow tones should be thinned by approximately 50 per cent with water. If diluted too much, the paint will run and form pools; if not diluted enough, it will build up and clog.

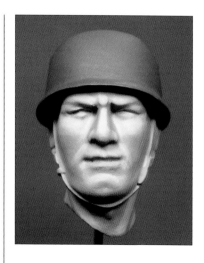

The second highlight goes over the same areas, but in a more restricted manner.

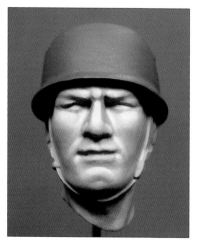

The third highlight. This is painted only on the most prominent areas.

The first shadow tone mix is made by adding Burnt Cadmium Red 814. It is laid on the zones receiving less light.

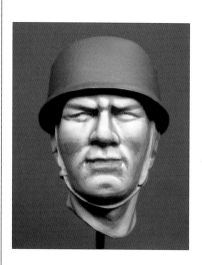

The second shadow covers a little less space in the same areas.

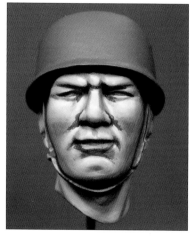

The deepest shadow is obtained by adding Black 950 to Burnt Cadmium Red. This tone goes on the most sunken areas.

The blending process: I use the same tones, but more diluted. I usually begin on the left side. I paint the eyes at this time too.

First, I lay the highlights on the 'upper' surfaces of the face: the upper cheeks, upper lip, chin tip, nose bridge and nostrils, mouth corners and eyelids. The first highlight is laid over the entire surface of these areas. The second follows, but is limited to a smaller area, the upper surfaces. The third covers a very small area in the uppermost areas of the surface. The fourth highlight is not used at this point. Because it is a very light colour, it is advisable to save adding this until the shadows are in place, so you can check the contrast – akin to a 'special effect' to be used if you feel it appropriate.

Next, I lay down the shadow tones on the appropriate areas: the eye sockets, nose sides and underneath, lower lip, under the cheeks, and the jaw. I begin with the first shadow, followed by the second, very much as per the highlights. The third shadow tone, Burnt Cadmium Red, is set aside momentarily. It has a very reddish hue, and would add too much 'warmth' to the face; I will use it

The moustache/beard stubble are painted by mixing some Black into each appropriate tone, in the area we are painting, be it highlight or shadow.

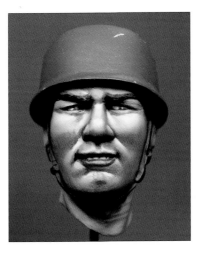

The 'five o'clock shadow' has been blended into the skin. I painted a blue iris in the eyes. Eyebrow definition is important for expression.

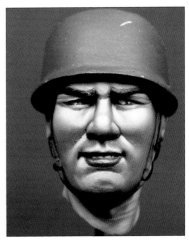

The blending process has been carried out on the right side of the face.

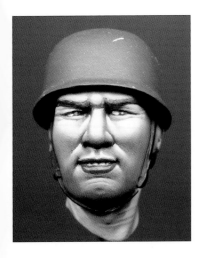

The stubble has already been blended in. I painted the lower lip with a pinkish red, obtained with Burnt Cadmium Red 814 and Basic Skintone 815. I apply three highlights.

The finished face. The eyebrows were highlighted with English Uniform 921, and underlined with Black.

The finished face. For the ears, I used the same mix as for the lower lip. The chinstrap is made of leather, which I imitated with Leather Brown 871, highlighted with Orange Brown 981 and shadowed with Black.

later on, to blend in the fourth shadow tone, which is only applied to the eye sockets, nose sides, under the lower lip, and around the jaw line.

Finally, I use black for the area on which the eyes will eventually be painted, and the mouth cavity.

Once basic highlights and shadows are in place, you should consider the well-defined face areas, and any expressive traits you are keen to replicate. Now you have a good idea of how the finished face will look, and can rectify any mistakes before actually carrying out the blending. This is the reason I prefer blocking in a limited number of highlight and shadow tones, including the extreme tones, instead of attempting to blend them from the beginning; doing so would make any flaws harder to anticipate and more difficult to correct.

The finished face. A weathered effect is suitable for the helmet. This was reproduced by applying Chocolate Brown 872, with a stabbing motion. The Luftwaffe eagle was painted by hand, in several grey hues.

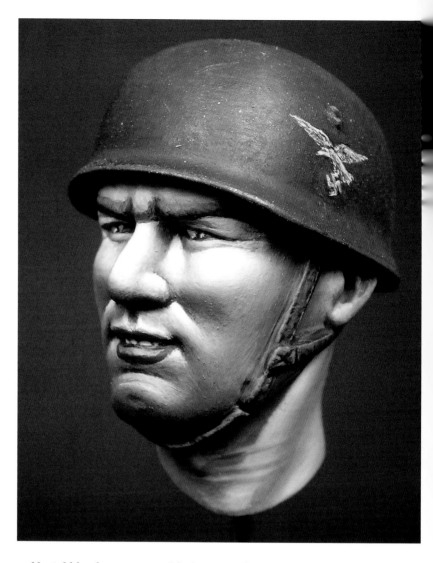

Next, I blend every tone with the ones adjacent to it. To this effect, colours have to be diluted even more, with 75 per cent water approximately. Every hue must be blended with those immediately before and after it in the luminescence scale. For instance, the base colour should be blended with the first highlight and first shadow tones, contiguous to it. The first highlight should blend with the base colour and second highlight tone; and so on.

Where two given tones meet, you will see a more or less ostensible border, which needs to be made to disappear. So, to blend the base colour with the first highlight, first dip the brush in the appropriate thinned base colour, and wipe the tip with a piece of absorbent paper to soak up most of the paint. Next, apply short brush strokes on the border line, until it is no longer visible. If instead of making the line disappear, you end up with a new one, it is because the paint is not sufficiently thinned. If you put too much paint on and cover up a given tone, you should paint the missing tone again.

This process should be repeated at every 'border' between tones, on every part of the face. Written down thus, it can appear long and complicated, but with a little practice, you will learn to do it automatically, without actually thinking about each step, and with great ease.

The fourth shadow tone technique is a little different. You will blend it with the second shadow tone – remember, the third tone was set aside. This blending will give a greyish hue; thus, you will now need the third shadow tone, blending it as an intermediate tone, thereby achieving a warmer hue in these transitional areas, and retaining, at the same time, the depth of the fourth shadow.

Normally, I start by blending the left half of the face, because, being right-handed I feel more comfortable working on that side; I complete the blending there before I turn to the right half. When blending, you are defining the key facial features and expressive traits, which have to be symmetric. So, by finishing one half first, you merely need to copy it onto the opposite half.

A 'five o'clock shadow', or a few days of beard growth, can be depicted by mixing some black paint into the tone we have previously applied on the place where stubble goes. Usually, this would be the first or second shadow tone on the jaw, and the second or third highlight tone on the moustache area. This is next blended by means of laying down sufficient levels of colour, just as for any other tone. I finish with some additional Black on the bottom part of the jaw.

Painting eyes begins by painting the eye socket in Black, which defines the eventual shape. Then, I paint a couple of small dots in Basic Skintone, in the right and left corners, inside the black contour. This creates a central black spot – the iris. Next, I lay a light blue highlight inside the iris, and finally a slightly off-centre tiny dot of Basic Skintone on the upper iris, imitating the reflection of light on the moist surface of a real eye.

Lips and ears are painted with a mix of Burnt Cadmium Red and Basic Skintone, to obtain a pinkish colour. Shadows and highlights are created with successively lighter and darker tones of each. In the inside of the mouth, I paint the teeth with a thin line of Basic Skintone; individual pieces are later defined with very fine black lines.

As a finishing touch, I reinforce the extreme highlights (on the upper-most cheek, nose wing and chin areas) with the fourth highlight tone, to increase contrast.

The helmet received a base coat of Luftwaffe Blue 816, which was lightened with Basic Skintone and shadowed with Dark Sea Blue 898. These tones are laid on with a stabbing motion, in order to suggest chipping and weathering effects, appropriate to such a piece of equipment. These effects are accentuated with Chocolate Brown 872, similarly applied.

Helmet decals were painted by hand; for instance, the eagle – first I drew the basic shape in light grey, then I filled it in, and ended by defining the details in black. There are no tricks to doing this: just patience and a steady hand.

Painting solid clothing colours

I paint unpatterned, solid clothing and fabrics with, essentially, the same techniques described for painting faces: I block in three highlight and three shadow tones, to achieve the desired contrast balance, and next I blend the transitions between colours. The main difference lies in the fact that a face always presents the same basic shapes (that is, you always have a nose, cheeks, ears, a chin, etc.), and so the highlights and shadows affect roughly the same areas. In addition, the colour palette remains generally unchanged – even if we vary the tones somewhat, the chromatic scale is similar (unless, of course, a race other than Caucasian is portrayed). In contrast, when painting clothing, you need to be familiar with many other colours; you have to study where to place highlights and shadows, and in what intensity these should be laid in order to obtain a correct contrast and a good definition of shapes.

What I do is to put the primed figure under a flexible lamp, and observe how light affects each area. Alternatively, I take a digital photograph of the figure and study these light and shadow effects on my computer screen. Either way, I carefully consider how to reproduce these effects on the figure.

Second-model jump smocks were made of a grey-green cloth; I examined photographs of preserved examples and noticed that this cloth had a high content of yellow fibres in its composition. I replicated this colour with a mix of Olive

The primed figure, ready to paint. Normally, it is advisable to assemble as many parts as possible before painting; in this case, the arms had to be kept separate, because they would get in the way when painting the chest area. It is important to ensure the separate parts fit properly, so a minimum of work is required when gluing them later on. A couple of holes were drilled in the figure's feet, through which wire rods are inserted. The figure is then provisionally placed on a temporary base, to ease handling.

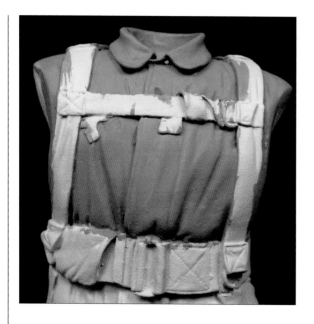

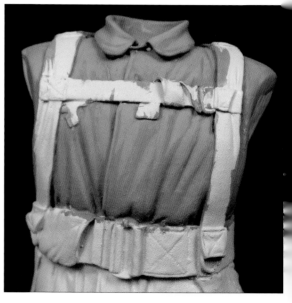

Solid colour techniques will be illustrated on the chest area. The base colour is mixed with Olive Grey 888, Grey Green 866 and Sunny Skintone 845. This is best applied in two or three thinned layers, covering the entire surface.

The first highlight, with Sunny Skintone 845 added to the base colour. Light colours tend to get clogged up, hence these must be well thinned.

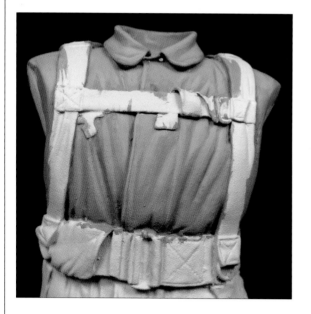

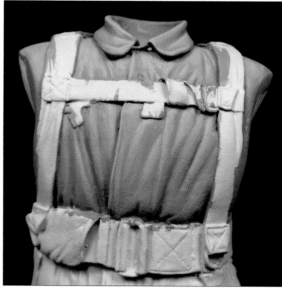

The second highlight, over the most prominent areas in every zone or crease.

The third highlight. You can already notice a sharpened contrast between highlighted and non-highlighted areas.

Grey 888, Grey Green 866 and Sunny Skintone 845, in a proportion of 40:40:20. I used Sunny Skintone for the highlight tones and Matt Black 950 for the shadows.

A very important factor when painting clothing is underlining. This operation consists of outlining, with a very dark (or even black on dark-coloured fabrics) colour, the shadow originated by a piece of clothing overlapping over another. In this case, for instance, the various parachute harness straps create a shadow on the clothes underneath – this shadow is imitated by underlining in

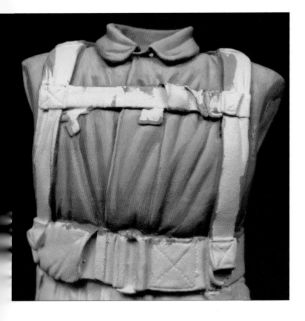

The first shadow, layered on the most sunken areas. Paint does not need to be as diluted with these darker hues.

The second shadow, applied where I want a really deep shadow. This tone will also outline those elements on top of the uniform, like parachute straps.

The blending process. I use heavily thinned mixes of every tone to blend each colour with that contiguous to it. This way, I soften the borders between colours, achieving a gradual transition.

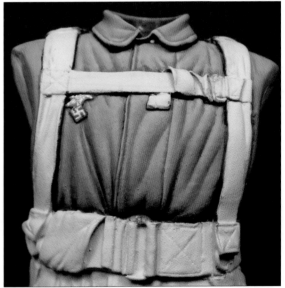

The blending process finished. It is advisable to paint the neighbouring elements, like the parachute straps in this case, to check if the contrast is appropriate. The Luftwaffe insignia must be painted as accurately as possible. In this scale, you can reproduce every detail, down to a well-defined swastika.

black the contact zone between both elements. This outlining must be subtle, and must appear well integrated with the adjacent tones, much like an extreme shadow tone.

When you work with thinned acrylics, it may happen that the paint acquires a satin or glossy look, either because of too great a dilution or too

The strapping finished. The base colour is Iraqi Sand 819 with Offwhite 820 in a 50:50 ratio; highlighted with more Offwhite, and shadowed with Chocolate Brown 872 added to the base mix. The impression of contrast should be consistent with the rest of the figure.

The completed torso, with arms and head added. The gloves were painted with Cadmium Maroon 859, adding Orange Brown 981 for highlights, and Black 950 for shadows.

The parachute attachment rope was made with a rope of the right thickness found in a naval modelling store. The kit's carbine hook was detailed with some photoetch bits and a new wire ring.

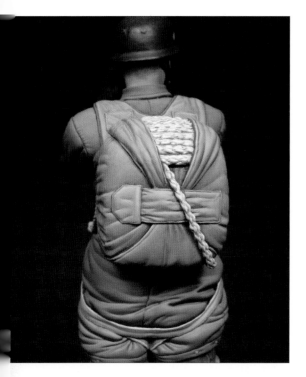

The RZ/16 parachute was painted with Khaki Grey 880 as a base colour, highlighted with Desert Yellow 977 and shadowed with Chocolate Brown 872. The lifeline rope was painted in a similar colour to that used for the strapping.

The metallic fittings were painted with non-metallic paints: Light Grey 990 for a base, highlighted with Offwhite 820 and shadowed with Black 950.

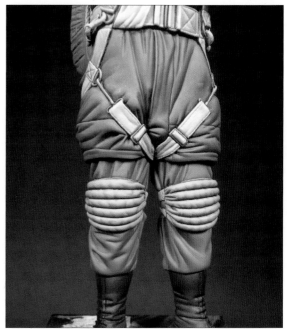

A different view of the finished torso.

A greenish field grey was chosen for the jump trousers, in order to increase the contrast with the smock. The base colour consists of Olive Grey 888 mixed with Khaki Grey 880. I added Iraqi Sand 819 for the highlights and Black 950 for the shadows.

I painted the knee pads with Iraqi Sand 819 mixed with German Camo Black Brown 822 in a 60:40 ratio, highlighted with additional Iraqi Sand and shadowed with German Camouflage Black Brown. I tried to suggest padding by means of painting heavily contrasting shadows and highlights. Referring to real examples of the item is very helpful.

The boots have a base of Leather Brown 871 mixed with Back 950, highlighted with Orange Brown 981. A little Iraqi Sand was added to the most prominent areas, suggesting a dusty surface, especially on those areas closest to the ground.

many brush strokes. It is paramount to avoid these effects, because clothing should look flat, unless intended to be silk or similar materials (unlikely for World War II figures). I favour Tamiya's X-21 Flat Base. This is a paste that is added to acrylic paint, ensuring it will dry absolutely flat. It has to be used in very limited amounts, because if you put too much of it on, the paint may well dry with a chalky, rough finish.

Groundwork

The terrain on which the figure stands was modelled with two-part epoxy putty, applied directly onto the base. This was rolled onto the surface in a uniform manner, and relief was created by pressing the putty with a textured stone. Do not forget to press the figure's feet into the surface, thus making a depression where it will properly fit.

Once the putty had cured, I laid down a coat of white glue, over which I applied different types of small stones and sand, short grass of several heights, and some strands of taller grass. In this particular case, I left a flattened area, where the supply container would rest its weight. When everything was dry, I painted every separate element with an airbrush, and applied the highlights by hand.

ABOVE The materials used to build the groundwork.

LEFT The base complete with its modelled groundwork, including some high grass. It is important to press the figure's feet into the groundwork, thus creating impressions where they will eventually fit. This will provide a realistic impression of 'weight'.

The basic groundwork colours were applied by airbrush. Note the space reserved for the container: this must look naturally settled on the grass, with a proper sense of 'weight'.

The painting finished. Some careful, selective dry-brushing can make the different elements stand out. I added some small roots in a random manner.

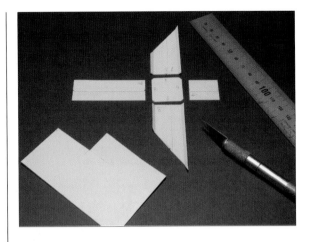

The airborne container broken down into its component plasticard pieces.

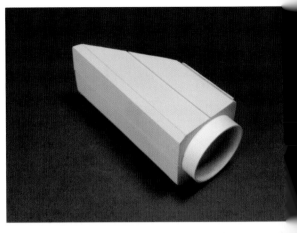

The assembled container. The anchoring hooks' protective fitting was made with a bottle cap cut to size.

The hinges were built with spare photoetch parts and plastic rod.

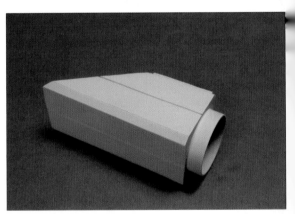

The container primed and ready to paint.

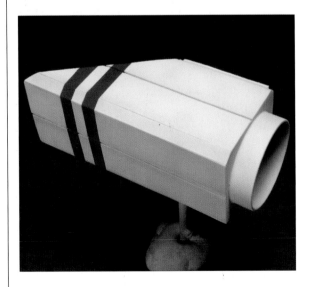

Identification bands were painted by airbrush on the masked surface.

The container in situ. Some weathering and chipping effects were added, with oils and acrylics.

The airborne container's section was built with 0.3mm-thick plasticard. I calculated the measurements by scaling up a container included in a 1/35 kit to 1/16 scale. The hinges were built with spare photoetch parts and plastic rod. The circular rim at the bottom came from a liquid soap bottle cap, which happened to be the right shape.

After priming the container, I airbrushed on a coat of white paint; next I used adhesive masking tape and added the red identification bands (containers were colour-coded according to their contents). Lastly, I mimicked a weathered, used look by a judicious application of chipped paint and scratch effects, using Chocolate Brown 872.

A couple of finishing touches: I added a reproduction of an issue of the wartime magazine *Signal*, featuring a jumping paratrooper on its cover. I found this image on the internet, reduced it to scale and printed it in high resolution. A few brown washes gave it a more realistic, used appearance. Another 'green devil' is visible in this vignette – a frog, expressly built in two-part putty for the occasion, providing a somewhat tongue-in-cheek, double meaning for the project!

BELOW AND NEXT PAGE **Views of the completed figure.**

ABOVE Finishing touches: the miniature facsimile of *Signal* magazine, and the other 'green devil', on the container.

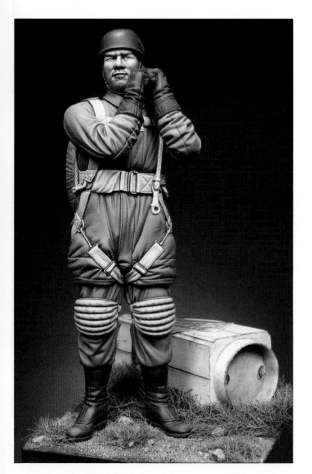

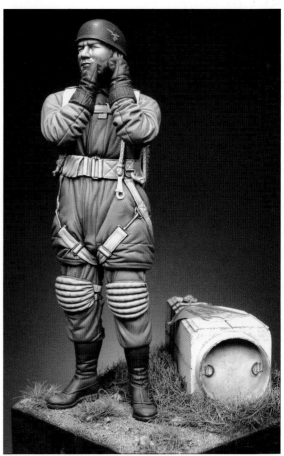

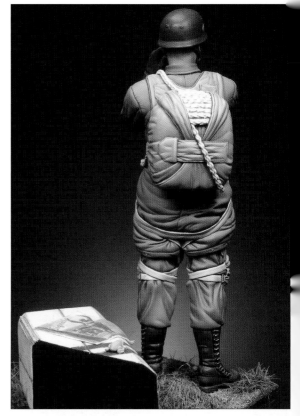
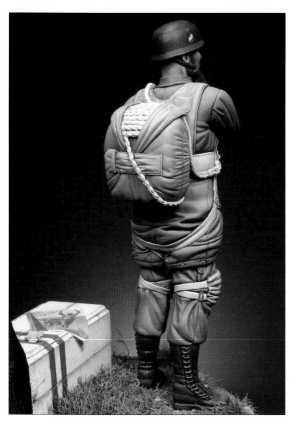

'Hunting party' Fallschirmjäger, Normandy, 1944

Subject:	Fallschirmjäger anti-tank team in mid-to-late war temperate weather uniforms
Project overview:	Camouflage painting techniques (Luftwaffe splinter and marsh patterns); basic vignette composition; introduction to architectural scenic bases.
Modellers:	Jaume Ortiz and Daniel Alfonsea
Skill level:	Advanced
Base figure:	Alpine Miniatures German Para with PzSchreck (no. 35020) and German Paratrooper (no. 35021)
Scale:	1/35
Additional materials used:	ABER no. 35D01, Tamiya X-21 Flat Base, Tamiya Surface Primer no. 87026
Paints:	Vallejo Model Colour: Matt Black 950, Brown Sand 876, Basic Skintone 815, Burnt Cadmium Red 814, Iraqi Sand 819, Deck Tan 986, Chocolate Brown 872, Mahogany Brown 846, Olive Grey 888, Blue Green 808, German Camo Orange Ochre 824, Mahogany Brown 846, Field Grey 830, Dark Yellow 978, Oily Steel 865, Leather Brown 871, Orange Brown 981, Glossy Black 861, Sunny Skintone 845

Introduction

After the Crete operation, the German paratrooper branch continued to expand, but these soldiers were mostly employed as elite shock troops (although several small-scale airborne actions were executed) and many of them were not even paratrooper qualified. They fought on every major front until the end of the conflict, in Africa, Russia, Italy, France, Holland, and in the defence of their homeland.

Beginning in 1941, the jump smock was manufactured in splinter camouflage pattern, a trend consolidated with the introduction of the third-model jump smock, which was made initially in hard-edged Luftwaffe splinter camouflage (distinct from the otherwise similar Army pattern, consisting of a less intricate combination of larger blocks); and later on, in the soft-edged variants, the latter also known as 'marsh' or 'tan-and-water' pattern, together with a less common intermediate 'semi-blurred edges' pattern – both of these identical to the Army pattern. The third-model smock had a more practical design, opening all the way down instead of being a step-in garment like its predecessor; a number of poppers at the lower hem allowed the gathering of the skirt around the legs, mimicking the second-model smock.

In this chapter, our target is to illustrate how to build a vignette with out-of-the box commercial figures, appropriately supported by groundwork suggestive of a particular geographic area – in this case Normandy; some space is given to basic composition and creating an architectural scenic base.

The selected figures, available as a pair from Alpine Miniatures, form a Panzerschreck tank-hunter team; the figures wear uniforms representative of

ABOVE An Oberjäger from FJR.9, 3.Fallschirmjäger Division, in an illustration from Osprey Publishing's Elite 11 *Ardennes 1944: Peiper and Skorzeny*.

ABOVE RIGHT The rocket launcher gunner, already primed. This figure is best painted without the weapon, because access to certain areas would be very difficult otherwise.

RIGHT The loader figure. As per usual, I drilled a couple of holes through its feet and inserted wire rod, fixing the figure to a provisional base, for ease of manipulation.

OPPOSITE The finished scene. I deliberately chose similar colours for the building and for the figures, in order to boost the effect of camouflage with the environment.

the mid-to-late war, as seen in every mild-weather front. The vignette idea is based on the idea that they are about to spring an ambush on some unsuspecting prey, from the cover of a typical Normandy manor house.

The features of this rural structure were culled from documentary references; the aim was to try to include a part of the building big enough for it to be readily identifiable and set the scene, while at the same time not overwhelming the figures with too much scenery. In addition, the fact that two levels are shown allows for an attractive composition with the figures, with the loader in the upper, and the gunner in the lower position.

Developing a storyline is paramount for a vignette to be effective. In this case, we have the loader, leaning to the side from his cover in the corner, as if warily peering at the oncoming threat; and the gunner in the foreground, in a more exposed position, both to have a clearer aim and to avoid the dangerous rocket backblast hitting the wall. Giving some thought to the 'what', 'who', 'why', 'when' and 'where' in a scene can really make it stand out.

The painting tutorials in this chapter are devoted to camouflage painting techniques, with two different types being discussed – the 'splinter' and the 'marsh' German patterns. We would like to thank Carles Elias for his help in building the architectural component of the vignette.

Painting camouflage patterns

When painting any form of camouflage pattern, there are several important factors that need to be taken into consideration: the design of the pattern, the colours involved, and the final look.

Design

Never improvise a camouflage pattern. Always try to recreate an actual design, with clear, recognizable features; base your work on a real example, and try to render it as faithfully as possible. There is a vast amount of information available at the modeller's disposal, be it in the form of specialized books, the internet, or collections, and we must draw on these, collating enough documents to ensure we can achieve a realistic result, true to the original.

We must carefully study the design, assimilating the diverse shapes, their colours and their distribution. Camouflage fabric patterns consist of a basic design that is successively repeated along the cloth – you have to reflect this repetition in your model too.

It may be that we have no clear view of every area of a given garment in a reference photo, but this is not a major problem if we have thoroughly understood the design, because then we will be able to piece together the missing parts and recreate the whole picture.

Another important consideration is that camouflaged garments are composed of a number of separate pieces that are sewn together. Hence, the pattern will not be continuous along the entire uniform. To the contrary, it will be interrupted by seams and will begin again, rarely matching the adjacent pieces; it can even change its orientation with respect to them.

Take the third-model smock that the subject figures here are wearing: it is formed by two back, two front and four arm major pieces, plus several smaller pieces like pocket flaps and other fittings. Although the camouflage pattern is common to all of them, it is not necessarily sewn following a common orientation, and of course seams break the pattern's continuity.

The gunner completed. The camouflage is a Luftwaffe 'splinter' pattern, this being the one most commonly found. It appears on the jump smock and the helmet cover.

Colours

Once again we must turn to our sources. We will see that there is no such thing as a unique, standard colour. The original clothing patterns obey specific regulations, but even in the raw material one finds discrepancies; add to this the circumstances related to its use, like weather conditions, fading, washing (or lack thereof), and other weathering factors, and a great variation in the colours a particular garment may present will result. This is something we must have in mind when replicating them, but we must also avoid overdoing the effect: the overall look has to be accurate according to our references.

Also, there must be harmony between the different colours, which should retain their integrity when weathered. To this effect, whenever feasible, include some common colour in the different base hue mixes; and try to use the same colours to prepare the highlights and shadow tones for these same basic hues.

The final look

As a concluding thought, do not forget that all of the above considerations must be coherent with the requirements of artistic representation: camouflaged garments have to be highlighted and shaded, and answer to the same luminescence concepts explained for face or plain clothing painting. Also, we must ensure an absolutely flat finish – any glossy areas will ruin the impression of realism of a camouflage uniform.

The Luftwaffe splinter pattern

I always follow five precise steps when painting this kind of camouflage.

First, I paint the colour that serves as a base for the pattern. This can be readily identified by a close look at the sources. For the present example, I mixed Iraqi Sand 819 with Deck Tan 986 and Chocolate Brown 872, in a 60:30:10 ratio, thus obtaining the desired yellowish grey. I follow this by outlining every seam or overlapping element that interrupts the camouflage design. This operation is very useful for emphasizing the places where the pattern finishes and begins anew. Any dark colour will do, but it is advisable to use one in the same colour range as the base colour.

Secondly, I reproduce the camouflage pattern. The splinter type consists of polygonal splotches, red brown and olive green in colour (see the Colour Chart No.1 on page 40); the former are larger and the latter are lodged inside them. So, I began with the brown ones.

Achieving straight lines is fairly laborious. Rarely will you get them right at the first attempt; you will need a good dose of patience, a brush with a sharp tip, and a steady hand. It is better to dilute the paint a little, so it flows better and the lines can be drawn without interruption. At this stage, I'm not worried if the shapes are not perfectly defined, instead I focus on keeping the design in scale and balanced. Further refining can be undertaken in the next step. Remember to add some Tamiya Flat Base to every colour to ensure a matt finish.

Thirdly, I add the highlights and shadows. Once the camouflage pattern is complete, it will not look very convincing: the colours will not be integrated and the result will appear plain and lifeless. Shadowing will change this. I use a highly controlled wash of

The loader finished. His smock is a different camouflage pattern, 'marsh' pattern 1943, characterized by blurred edges.

The 'splinter' base colour. It is a yellowish grey, which I mixed with Iraqi Sand 819 and Deck Tan 986. Do not forget to put some Tamiya Flat Base into the mix.

Outlining the different elements that will break up the camouflage pattern. Any dark colour would be adequate, although it is better to use one already present in this particular pattern's colour composition; in this case, Chocolate Brown 872.

I painted the brown blocks with Mahogany Brown 846 and Chocolate Brown 872. I referred to photographs of the actual garment and copied its design. Don't worry if the shapes are not perfectly defined; this can be improved later. The objective is to obtain a design as similar as possible, globally, to the real one.

Chocolate Brown 872; the paint should be very thin, with a consistency akin to that of dirty water, and some Flat Base to prevent glossiness. This wash is applied over the entire garment, not just the folds and wrinkles, and will help integrate the different colours. Then, I selectively apply the same wash to every wrinkle, two or three times, until satisfied with the intensity of the shadow. In the areas of particularly deep shadow, I add some black to the wash. When the shadowing is finished, the original colours will look somewhat dulled.

As a fourth step, to recover the vividness of the colours, I highlight the upper surfaces of the folds, and other areas where this would be appropriate because of exposition to the source of light, with the same colours initially used to paint the splotches. I then prepare a maximum highlight tone for every colour, which I apply on the most prominent areas of every fold. This process calls for diluted paint, as explained for the solid colour highlights. At this stage, I also redefine any shape which may have been blurred by the previous steps.

Fifthly, I paint on the 'raindrop' fine lines that are so characteristic of this camouflage. Check your illustrated sources again to find out which areas have to be painted so, because not all of the design features the raindrops. I used pure Olive Grey 888, well thinned. The degree of dilution has to be constantly checked by test-painting on a white sheet before actually putting the brush onto the figure. It is preferable to paint very subtle, almost invisible, fine lines, than to have them too thick and bold – hence the need for well-diluted paint.

When the camouflage is finished, I paint up any straps and equipment, to check if the overall contrast is correct.

The marsh pattern 1943

The same process applies for painting this pattern as for the above one. The base colour in this case is a mustard yellow, which I created mixing German Camo Orange Ochre 824 with Chocolate Brown 872 and Iraqi Sand 819, in a 60:20:20 ratio.

Next come the green blocks, placed in their appropriate locations. The green tone is a mix of Olive Grey 888, Blue Green 808 and Deck Tan 986.

A rear view of the smock, with the basic design done. You have to constantly check that the balance and proportion between the different coloured blocks is maintained.

Next I applied a very controlled Chocolate Brown 872 wash, in order to unify the colours and shade them a little. You must avoid blotching the paint, as this would be detrimental to the effect. You should apply a stronger wash in the deeper creases; it may even be appropriate to add some Black to the wash, for the deepest crevices to stand out.

The highlighting follows. The original colours, darkened by the previous process, are recovered by means of applying each one of the base colours on those areas receiving more light. Finally, some more Deck Tan 986 is added to each colour, thus creating lighter tones that are layered on the most prominent areas – those more exposed to the light source.

The last task is to patiently paint the 'rain' lines, one by one, using well-thinned Olive Grey 888. If the paint is too thick, the lines will look too bold; if too thin, they will look too blurred. You must find the exact point of dilution by trial and error, testing the effect on paper or card before you tackle the figure. Soaking up the excess paint with tissue paper is useful.

The smock's frontal part, completed. The combination of selective washes and individual spot highlighting results in a very attractive three-dimensional effect. I usually paint the adjacent or overlapping elements, to check the contrast.

A frontal view of the finished figure. I attached the Panzerschreck once the head was already painted and fixed in place.

A side view. The trousers' colour base is Field Grey 830, highlighted with Basic Skintone 815, and shadowed with Black 950.

The Panzerschreck was painted in Dark Yellow 978. The weathering and chipping effects were accomplished with washes of Chocolate Brown 872 and Oily Steel 865.

The face was painted following the steps and colours described in the previous chapter. The helmet cover was painted in the same manner as the smock.

The 'marsh' pattern 1943 base colour: a mix of German Camo Orange Ochre 824, Chocolate Brown 872 and Iraqi Sand 819, plus Flat Base, to ensure a matt finish, especially needed in camouflage garments.

Outlining the different pieces of the smock. We must have a very clear idea of where the various seams break the camouflage pattern.

Painting the green and brown spots. In this pattern, the green predominates. This design was common to the Army, unlike the specific Air Force 'splinter' pattern the other figure shows.

Blurring the spots' edges. By mixing the green and the brown with the base colour, we obtain an intermediate hue, which, when applied on each spot's contours, gives an 'aurora' effect. This blurring is a defining feature of this camouflage.

Once the Chocolate Brown 872 wash has been applied, I proceed to highlight the more prominent areas. Note how the wash has harmonized the colours and has increased the diffuse effect in the spots' contours.

Adding even darker washes to the deepest creases will create a more effective volume definition. I used Sunny Skintone 845, added to every basic colour, for highlighting. Once again, I outlined every neighbouring or overlapping element, with very thin Black paint.

The camouflage design is as per the Heer splinter pattern, just with inverted colours: the green splotches are more numerous and larger than the red-brown splotches (see Colour Chart No.2 on page 40 for the colour mixes).

I went through the same steps explained previously, keeping in mind that, although similar, the splotches for this pattern vary in shape and size. The most evident difference is that the edges are not hard, but diffuse. I prepared a 50:50 mix of the base and the green colours, obtaining an intermediate hue. This was

The finished back part. The belting and the pistol holster were painted in Leather Brown 871 mixed with Black 950, highlighted with Orange Brown 981. Weathering and fading was suggested with pure Orange Brown, applied to the edges of these leather pieces.

Lastly, I painted the 'rain' lines, characteristic of this pattern too, with well-diluted Olive Grey 888.

The frontal part. Note that the same camouflage design is apparent on both sides of the garment. As already explained in the main text, these patterns actually have a periodically repeating design, and this particular aspect must be evident in our figures too.

The completed figure. Accessories need to be carefully painted too, if you want a lifelike finish.

The completed figure.

The completed figure from the rear.

applied, well diluted, on the borders between each splotch edge and the basic colour, as if to fuse the colours together: in this way, I achieved a good imitation of the diffuse borders in the real thing. The areas where brown and green splotches are in contact were similarly treated, and with the same colour mix.

Once I finished with this, I proceeded to the highlighting and shadowing, as per the Luftwaffe splinter pattern: a wash of heavily thinned Chocolate Brown 872 was applied all over the garment, followed by a darker wash (with Black added to Chocolate Brown) on the deepest recesses, then highlighting

I imitated the texture of the rifle's wooden parts with very fine lines in various brown hues. The metal parts were reproduced with a mix of Chocolate Brown 872 and Glossy Black 861.

with the original colours, and ending with a very light touching up using the base colours plus Sunny Skintone 845.

Groundwork: building a structure

When tackling the construction of a building, research is no less important than when painting figures. There is a big difference between an invented building, more or less reminiscent of the architecture proper to a given region, and a building based on photographs of actual constructions in that region.

You do not have to necessarily copy an actual building, but you should at least consider what the predominating architectural characteristics are for a particular region, what materials are used, what the most common colours of these materials are, and whatever useful details you can incorporate into your model, in order to prompt recognition of a characteristic style at first sight by the viewer.

In this case, we wanted to depict a typical Normandy manor house. To this end, we studied a great number of images of farms and rural buildings, selecting those most outstanding. For instance, the colour of the stone, the use of tiles as a wall revetment, and the wooden elements, are all indicative of the Normandy landscape.

Firstly, it is advisable to draw sketches of the building, to make sure that any details are not overlooked when actually building it. Next, make a cardboard mock-up, to check sizes and the scale with respect to the figures.

The next step for us is to begin by building the lower part of the structure, using 2mm-thick cardboard. The stone walls and floors are reproduced with fine grain compacted cork sheet, 3mm thick, except for the stone steps, made of thicker 5mm sheet.

Prior to assembling these pieces, you need to texture the cork surfaces. This can be done with a metal file, until you obtain an adequate texture. Next, scrub it with wire wool, to smooth the surface and remove loose particles. Now the individual stone pieces are cut out: do not attempt to keep them uniform – the idea is to have differently sized and shaped pieces, which are later assembled, much like a puzzle.

Wall and roof tiles are cut from 0.5mm cardboard sheet. Again, avoid too much uniformity: make them slightly different but with generally similar measurements. The door and wall beams are made from balsa wood, textured with a wire brush.

When all the cork and cardboard pieces are in place on the structure, the empty areas between each component must be filled with plaster; a spatula is a suitable tool for this. Just spread the plaster all over the surface, and then remove the excess material with the same tool.

Meanwhile, you can prepare the groundwork for the base. Glue down a piece of cork sheet, taking care to keep clear the area where the building is going to be later. Its surface is then covered with dirt and little rocks, plus several strands of static grass, cut to irregular lengths and randomly set to simulate vegetation.

The ivy plant is from a photoetch sheet, marketed by Aber. To achieve realistic results, take the time to carefully bend and twist every separate leaf. The flowerpots were fashioned from the protective caps of hypodermic needles, cut to the required size. The flowers are real, picked from a garden; airbrushing some varnish on will keep the flowers from drying out.

The ground and the house were painted with acrylics, except for the wooden parts, for which oil paints were used instead.

Building architectural elements. Firstly, the building is drawn, in order to achieve a clear idea of its shape and volume. This is followed by building a cardboard model, to check the dimensions with the figures and the base.

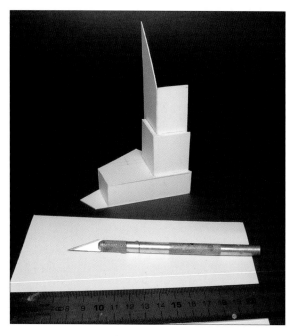

34 | The building is made of 2mm-thick cardboard.

The basic shapes completed.

Texturing the surface with a wire brush.

Smoothing the surface. At this stage, any loose cork particles are removed too.

The stones are cut out of 3mm-thick cork board. Do not attempt to make them all alike – a little variation will add realism.

The stones' edges are ground down with the wire brush, avoiding perfect angles and excessive uniformity.

The cardboard structure is lined with the cork pieces, on the walls and floors.

Individual tiles were fashioned from 0.5mm-thick cardboard, and glued in place.

The completed roof. The excess at the edges was carefully removed with scissors.

ABOVE A view of the building, with all of its elements in place.

LEFT The door and the beams were built from balsa wood, textured with a wire brush.

The empty spaces between the stones are filled with plaster, using a spatula.

The finished building.

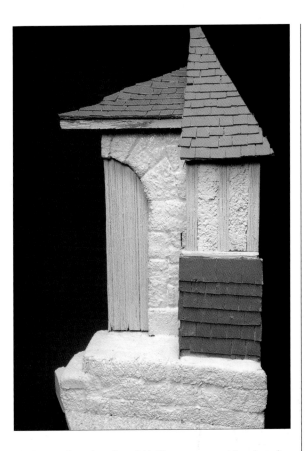

The basic colours have been laid. These were specially selected for the figures' camouflaged uniforms to merge with, thus better integrating the different elements that form the scene.

ABOVE The terrain is shaped with a piece of cork board, from which a space for the building has been cut out. Next, fine sand and small stones are sprinkled on this; some high grass, made by Noch, is added, together with some strands of dried seaweed.

RIGHT The terrain is painted with an airbrush; after this, some selective touches of dry-brushing enhance the ground and plants.

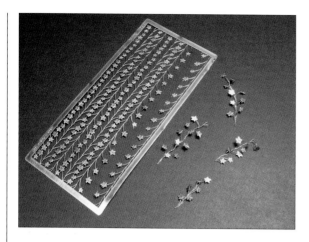

ABOVE Some ivy is placed on the wall, to enliven the area. This is a photoetch part by Aber, improved by means of folding and twisting every individual leaf at different angles.

RIGHT View of the completed groundwork. As a finishing touch, two flowerpots were strategically placed; these were made from the caps of hypodermic needles. The flowers are real ones, varnished after picking, to avoid them drying out. Note the subtle detail of one of the pots being broken, to suggest someone has just knocked it over.

BELOW AND OPPOSITE Views of the finished vignette.

Colour Chart No.1: Luftwaffe splinter pattern

Base colour

	Iraqi Sand 819	Deck Tan 986	Chocolate Brown 872
Mixing ratio:	60 per cent	30 per cent	10 per cent

Red Brown

	Mahogany Brown 846	Chocolate Brown 872	
Mixing ratio:	70 per cent	30 per cent	

Medium Green

	Olive Grey 888	Blue Green 808	Deck Tan 986
Mixing ratio:	50 per cent	30 per cent	20 per cent

Colour Chart No.2: marsh pattern 1943

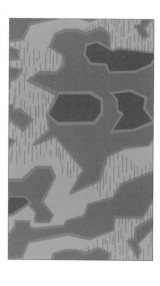

Base colour

	German Camo Orange Ochre 824	Chocolate Brown 872	Iraqi Sand 819
Mixing ratio:	60 per cent	20 per cent	20 per cent

Red Brown

	Mahogany Brown 846	Chocolate Brown 872	Sunny Skintone 845
Mixing ratio:	60 per cent	20 per cent	20 per cent

Medium Green

	Olive Grey 888	Sunny Skintone 845	Chocolate Brown 872
Mixing ratio:	60 per cent	30 per cent	10 per cent

'Say "Cheese"!': Fallschirmjäger in Italy, 1943

Subject:	Fallschirmjäger in tropical uniforms
Project overview:	Figure conversion techniques. Tropical uniform painting. Vignette design: composition, interaction.
Modellers:	Jaume Ortiz and Daniel Alfonsea
Skill level:	Master
Base figure:	Elisena German Paratrooper 1941 (no. 10120) and Afrikakorps Private 1942 (no. 10125)
Scale:	54mm
Additional materials used:	Milliput Silver White two-part modelling putty, Tamiya X-21 Flat Base, Tamiya Surface Primer no. 87026
Paints:	Matt Black 950, Brown Sand 876, Basic Skintone 815, Burnt Cadmium Red 814, Desert Yellow 977, Orange Brown 981, Ice Yellow 858, Buff 976, German Camouflage Black Brown 822, Khaki Grey 880, Olive Grey 888, Mahogany Brown 846, Chocolate Brown 872, Leather Brown 871, Orange Brown 981

Introduction

From 1942 onwards, Fallschirmjäger were engaged in the Mediterranean Theatre, from the time of El Alamein up to the last battles of the Afrika Korps in Tunisia. From there, they went on to Sicily and then to the Italian mainland, where they remained until the end of World War II. In Italy they won what is possibly their best-known battle honour, that of the hard-fought Montecassino campaign.

The main aim of this chapter is to highlight the tropical uniforms issued to the paratroopers. As a matter of fact, no single item was specific to the airborne arm – tropical items were designed for the Luftwaffe as a whole, which the paratroopers used on their own or combined with their special equipment. The lightweight (LW) tropical outfit consisted of a two-piece uniform, plus matching headdress in various models.

Apparently, there was a plan to produce a tan-coloured jump smock, supposedly to be first used in the planned invasion of Malta, an operation that would be eventually cancelled. This would have been the only purpose-designed tropical smock. These did not make it to full-scale production, and were certainly not issued in any significant numbers. Consequently, Fallschirmjäger deployed in the Mediterranean wore the general issue camouflage smocks.

From a modelling perspective, this chapter also takes us a stage further; our objective is to exemplify how to adapt commercial figures to our purposes, modifying both uniform details and poses, in this case creating a vignette where interaction between components is especially important to tell a story. We have selected two 54mm metal figures (which are sold separately) as the basis for this project. The step-by-step painting sequence explores a variant of the splinter pattern: the design is the same, but the colours of the camouflage blocks are reversed, green being the dominant colour instead of red brown.

Our vignette portrays a pair of Fallschirmjäger NCOs, freshly awarded the Iron Cross Second Class (*Eiserne Kreuz II*) in a frontline ceremony, celebrating in an Italian trattoria, and proudly displaying their badges of courage.

The Iron Cross Second Class was the lowest level of the famous German Iron Cross medal. It was awarded in large numbers, with about 2.3 million recipients. This decoration was chosen because it was so widespread, in order to depict a generic event with anonymous protagonists. The Iron Cross Second Class itself was worn only on the day it was actually awarded; later, only the ribbon was displayed, on the second buttonhole or at an equivalent position.

OPPOSITE PAGE From left to right, a Hauptmann, a Feldwebel, and a Jäger in tropical dress in North Africa 1942–43; this illustration is from Osprey Publishing's Men-at-Arms 139: *German Airborne Troops*.

Tropical uniforms

The soldiers in the scene represent two typical paratroopers in a hot climate: one wears the two-piece tropical uniform, and the so-called 'Hermann Meyer' cap; and the other the regular smock over the tropical trousers, and a lightweight sidecap.

Converting figures

I selected two fine Elisena 54mm figures for this project. As is commonly the case, the figures were in fact larger than 54mm, averaging 65mm to the top of the head.

The sergeant

The most straightforward conversion was for the Paratrooper 1941 (no. 10120) figure. Basically, it entailed remodelling the jump trousers into tropical ones.

'Say "Cheese"!' – the completed vignette.

The original Elizena paratrooper figure. It being a paratrooper already, the uniform details will need less alteration, but the final result is significantly different compared to the starting model.

43

The jump trousers were converted into tropical trousers; these are considerably bulkier, so I built them, up, over the original surface. At the same time, I modified the balance of volume for the right leg, suggesting a more relaxed stance.

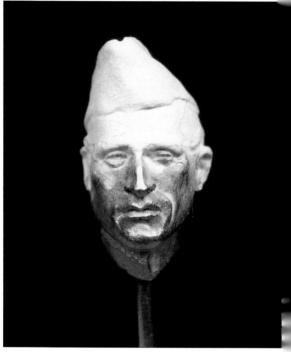

I modelled a side cap on a replacement head. First I had to rebuild the top of the head, because it had a different type of headgear, which I discarded. Over this, I applied the basic form of the new cap, taking care to reproduce the correct shape and checking it was appropriately placed at an angle. The details would follow later.

These were wider, and had a characteristically baggy look. The leg pose almost matched my intentions, so I just built up the trousers with Milliput, more or less following the original shape; however, I took the chance to modify the right leg's volume, suggesting a more curved bend of the limb underneath the trousers, making the stance look more relaxed. I added the lower part of the thigh pocket, showing under the smock.

As it comes, the smock is a second-model example. I planned to paint it in a camouflage pattern, so I updated it with third-model features, by the addition of a single pistol pocket and a shovel tab in the back skirt.

The original head was not adequate for my purposes, so I substituted it with another from the same manufacturer, and modelled the tropical side cap (*schiffchen* – meaning 'little ship') on top of it. According to regulations, this was supposed to be worn squarely on the head, but in reality it was almost universally pinched (or sewn) at the crown and canted over to the right ear, in an angle according to the wearer's taste. The head was attached at a particular angle, as if looking at the other figure, reinforcing the interaction between them.

The face itself received some attention: its features were remodelled to suggest a slightly scornful expression.

The right arm is a conversion of the one in the box. I cut a wedge at the elbow area and increased its bend; then I reconfigured the arm insertion area. Both these actions entailed some reconstruction of the clothing drapes. For the hand, I removed the sub machine gun handle it was holding, and remodelled the palm and fingers as required.

The left arm, in contrast, was scratchbuilt, its intended pose being too different from the original to justify its use. In fact, this arm was crucial to the

The trousers' shape is basically defined by now. The right arm was converted from the one in the box. At this stage, the elbow area has already been remodelled; the shoulder insertion point had to be appropriately reworked too.

Now that the right arm's conversion is done, it's time to scratchbuild the left one. The hand was linked to the body with a wire skeleton, and the arm's pose was carefully checked, to ensure a good adaptation, with the other figure. Then a very basic muscular form was modelled on it, fixing the pose.

The conversion is at an advanced stage here. The left arm's sleeve was modelled with a view to some of its surface (in the lower arm) being in contact with the other figure's back; and the sleeve's cloth would be pressed upon here.

The relevant areas were given attention before the putty had completely set, to ensure a tight fit. Note the head is set at a particular angle: this is important as body language and interaction are closely related.

interaction between the figures, it being over the other paratrooper's shoulder and had to be seamlessly adapted to it – scratchbuilding was the only option. By the way, it is a good idea to model the pose you have in mind for your figure in front of a mirror, especially if it is ambitious or unconventional, to make sure it is natural, and to use this a reference. Do not 'deduce' or 'guess' poses: more often than not, the result will be unconvincing.

First I made a basic wire armature, to which I attached a suitable hand from a different figure. This armature was based on an anatomical diagram, which I had previously converted to the right scale, to keep its proportions and joints correct. Next, I checked this armature in relation to the companion figure, and fixed the arm's position, building up a basic muscular volume over the wire skeleton. The following step was to model the sleeve. I constantly checked with the anatomical diagram, to avoid 'shifting' the joints; and with the other figure, taking care the arm of one fitted the back and shoulder of the other well.

I made a pair of rank patches for the arm, as used on smocks and other garments, to show sergeant (*feldwebel*) insignia.

For the Iron Cross, I made use of a Dragon 1/35-scale photoetch Knight's Cross; being a larger medal, it is the ideal size to represent the Knight's Cross in Elisena's larger figures.

The staff sergeant

The other figure was to display both the tropical uniform and some badges commonly worn by Fallschirmjäger. Other than the Luftwaffe eagle and rank patches, no insignia would be worn on jump smocks, except when on parade and for special occasions; so, I decided my staff sergeant (*stabsfeldwebel*) would have a different look.

The very first Luftwaffe units arriving in Africa used Army tropical uniforms, but soon they were issued their own pattern, which saw widespread service. As a source for my conversion, I took figure no. 10125, an Army Afrika Korps infantryman, and 'transferred' him to the Luftwaffe by means of a conversion.

The head is the one supplied with the kit. I had to slightly alter the area around the right corner of the mouth, where a cigar would be inserted later. Besides that, I sawed off the peaked cap, and scratchbuilt a 'Hermann Meyer' cap in its place. The 'tropical field visor cap' was regulation issue, but the troops rechristened it with Hermann Göring's irreverent nickname. This cap has some peculiarities compared to the well-known *schirmütze* Army or Luftwaffe service cap. Its top is definitely larger, and, not being stiffened, it has a softer appearance; also, its visor is not leather but cloth, and is of greater dimensions. It had a leather chinstrap attached. This item was often reversed to the rough side, to match the cap better. I studied photographs of the actual headgear, trying to capture its look.

The legs received a treatment similar to that described for the sergeant, building up their volume to the desired style. In this instance, the whole thigh pocket is visible.

I had to rebuild the major part of the tunic skirt, because of the changes to the right arm's pose. The original one was, in any case, far too short at the back, and lacked the central slit.

I changed the arms too. First, the rolled sleeves had to go; I removed the sleeves, leaving the arms bare. The left arm's pose was fine, so I just 'dressed' it. The right one was the object of a more substantial reworking. It was fundamental to pull the pose through, because the hand showing off the Iron Cross constituted the central point in the scene. If you try it yourself, you will see it is a somewhat complex stance, even involving the shoulder (which I had to build up a little); I found it easier to remove the entire elbow section, and part of the upper arm, linking the remaining bits with wire, in order to be able to set the arm provisionally in place and play around with it until I was satisfied. At that moment I fixed the pose and added back the muscular volume. I did not 'dress' this arm in place; because of the angle of the lower arm, I had to model a hollow

ABOVE Note both arms had their sleeve detail removed, leaving them bare. The right arm's pose was kept as it was, but I had to carry out major changes to the left one. In this photograph, you can see the new scratchbuilt cap is almost finished.

LEFT The staff sergeant in tropical uniform was based on Elisena's Afrika Korps Infantryman, here in an excellent out-of-the box rendering by our friend Pedro Ramirez.

The new sleeve has been modelled over the bare left arm. You can see that every unwanted Army insignia and badge has been removed from the figure, to be substituted with Air Force equivalents.

A rear view. The right arm is basically complete now too. The rear skirt area would later be completely remodelled. The original figure was designed to have some equipment over it, very much hiding this area; I discarded the equipment, so I had to rebuild the skirts accordingly, adapting the cloth to the new situation.

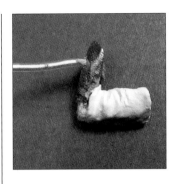

I found it easier to 'dress' the right lower arm before attaching it to the figure, especially because it had to have a hollow effect. I provisionally inserted a length of wire into the basic arm, to ease manipulation.

sleeve, this detail being visible at the raised cuff end. I rolled a very thin sheet of Milliput, cut it roughly to size, and draped it over the lower arm, thus creating the effect; when the putty had cured a little, I put the arm in the desired position, pressing it on the chest area to adapt the sleeve to the surface. The hand is plastic and came from the spares box.

The Army's *litzen* collar insignia were eliminated; I did not substitute Luftwaffe patches, these being very rarely applied to the tropical tunic. A LW-style eagle took the place of the Army's one on the right breast. I rebuilt the right shoulder strap, and added *waffenfarbe* piping and *stabsfeldwebel* rank pips.

The left chest pocket underwent some reworking. I filed off the flap and added some volume to the pocket, to suggest it was filled: you will notice a fistful of cigars emerging from the opening.

I removed the Infantry Assault Badge on the left pocket, and modelled instead the more proper Luftwaffe Ground Assault Badge, and the Paratrooper Qualification Badge. The figure had, in addition, a Wound Badge (the lower class in black), which I left, this being an appropriate award. As a final touch, I added the Kreta (Crete) campaign cuffband. This would be a fairly common set of insignia for a Fallschirmjäger veteran. Study your references to ensure the combination is plausible for a given soldier; and take care to place them correctly, in the regulation position and in the right order of precedence (combat badges rank above qualification badges, but below decorations). This was not always strictly adhered to, so it is advisable to check contemporary photographs for deviations.

The major putty remodelling work has already been done. The new areas are in a rough state, which will be further defined and detailed. Note I only modelled part of the right lower pocket – this area would eventually be mostly hidden by a map case. You can see the right sleeve is hollow at the cuff.

A rear view at the same stage of construction. The fact that the left hand is in the trouser pocket influences the drapes of the left skirt, which I had to remodel going over the arm, trying to keep the transition with the front skirt area smooth.

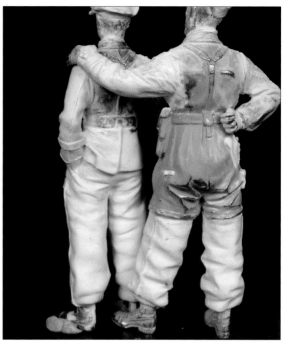

ABOVE LEFT AND RIGHT Checking the composition. Both figures are nearly finished. You may notice some smaller details that were added when the main work was done, like new badges and insignia, are a different colour. I put some plasticine in the putty mix, just enough to change the colour – the putty properties do not vary appreciably. I do this when I need some contrast with the previously remodelled surface – this helps me on the definition of new detail. At this stage, both figures were undergoing facial changes, to modify their expression to suit my needs.

From the above explanations, I hope you can see how the research phase really pays off – spending some time on this minimizes the possibility of your committing accuracy-related mistakes; but it is equally important to understand that familiarizing yourself with the subject will give you a wealth of ideas that can be incorporated in your project, making it more out-of-the-ordinary, more original, more personal – and thus all the more fulfilling.

As already noted, the figures' composition was constantly checked. Note how the relationship between both subjects is reinforced by body language, namely the subtle angle of the head of the first figure, looking at the second figure, and the physical contact of the lower left arm and hand of the first figure in contact with the shoulder of the second figure. These touches really do link the individual figures together in what could be called a sculptural group, making the composition more powerful and appealing.

Painting the figures

In this chapter, I will not discuss the techniques for painting solid or patterned uniforms, because these are very similar to those addressed in the preceding two projects. I would like, instead, to deal with some concepts worth noting when painting figures that share the same base, in a vignette or diorama; and how to use paint as an additional tool in the composition.

The faces

In this vignette, the figures' faces are very important, and they will immediately draw the viewer's attention. The protagonists are in the middle of a celebration for the awards bestowed on them, and their expressions must transmit pride and joy.

By means of careful painting, the sculpted traits on a given figure's face can be enhanced, or even altered, to convey different feelings. Obviously, if the

A close-up view of the first figure's face. I painted some exaggerated wrinkles to 'force' a smile, especially around the mouth, cheeks and eyes. It is worth the effort to carefully reproduce the cap insignia, for a realistic result.

A close-up view of the second figure's face. Again, I forced the smile by 'pulling' up the left lip corner. The cigars are tiny putty sausages, painted in dark brown; some touches of light grey at the tip give a convincing ash effect.

features already present are adequate for the intended expression, our task will be that much easier. In this case, converting the figures included a certain degree of facial remodelling, mainly centred on adapting the mouths and surrounding areas to the action of holding a couple of respectable cigars.

There was a modest attempt at changing their expressions during the conversion stage, but in truth it is through the painting process that this change can be made, and a joyful and proud feeling conveyed. Thus, by strengthening the cheeks' wrinkles, and pulling the mouth's corners upwards, with *trompe l'oeil* contrast painting effects I created a smile. I suggested some squinting of the eyes, which, together with a raised eyebrow, result in a somewhat scornful complacent expression. A little delicate outlining of the mouth contour, and a point of highlighting on the upper lip, intensify the sensation that the cigar is naturally accommodated in the mouth. For both figures, I tried to exaggerate the expressive traits by painting some wrinkles on the cheeks, at the corners of the mouths, around the eyes and on the cheekbones.

Colours

Independently of the particular colours of each of the figures featured in a vignette or diorama, we can create 'sympathy' between these colours with the use of some 'talisman' hues, which will unify and harmonize the whole.

When the figures are wearing similarly coloured uniforms, an effective technique is making use of the same basic colour for all of them, but changing the tones chosen for the highlighting and shadowing effects on each figure.

For example, in our scene, both figures wear the same kind of sand-coloured trousers. I selected Desert Yellow 977 as the basic colour, but, on applying the highlights, I used Ice Yellow 858 for the foreground figure, and Buff 976 for the one in the background. On the other hand, the same tone, German Camouflage Black Brown 822, was picked for the shadows. This procedure results in a very similar general tone, but with subtle differences, for each garment, allowing them to combine nicely due to the common colours.

The same technique can be used to our advantage to harmonize figures with different uniforms; to this effect, we will pick our 'talisman' colours for the lighting effects.

The first figure, complete. The tropical web gear was painted in Brown Sand 876, shaded with Chocolate Brown 872. In order to make the various badges and decorations stand out, some careful painting is in order. It is not often that you see this combination of insignia on a figure, hence it is appropriate to take some time with these eye-catching details.

The second figure, finished. The camouflage is a variant of the splinter pattern, particularly notable for the different colour distribution.

As a case in point, take our figures again: the one in the foreground wears a tunic painted in Khaki Grey 880, then highlighted with the addition of Basic Skintone 815 to this base colour, then shadowed by mixing some Chocolate Brown 872 into it. The other figure is clad in the jump smock, this time showing a different 'splinter' camouflage pattern consisting of green and brown blocks, with the green predominating, on a more yellowish ground. The basic colour I created mixing Desert Yellow 977 with Buff 976 in a 50:50 ratio. The green spots are a mix of Olive Grey 888 and Buff 976 in a 70:30 ratio; and the brown ones Mahogany Brown 846 with Desert Yellow 977 in a 70:30 ratio.

As previously explained, once the basic design is painted, each colour must be separately shadowed first, and then highlighted. The shadowing was done with very thin washes of Chocolate Brown 872, that is, the same hue used for the shadows of the companion figure. This will ensure the tonal unification of both figures. The highlights were made by adding a little Buff 976 to each basic hue.

Achieving contrast

This is another important element to consider when painting various figures for the same scene. The level of contrast applied to each figure needs to be the same, or very similar between them, in order to achieve a continuity between the various elements in the composition; and to avoid the feeling that each figure has been painted separately.

'Contrast' means the difference between the maximum highlights and the maximum shadows. Hence, it is advisable to use the same range of hues, or at

I tried to render a softer pattern of contrast in the trousers, suggestive of the light fabric these are made of; also, the baggy cut is not so susceptible to tight wrinkles.

This lightweight leather gear is often seen used by paratroopers. I painted it in Orange Brown 981, highlighted with Desert Yellow 977.

least hues of similar intensity, to paint the diverse garments the different figures are wearing. This will very much bracket the maximum levels for shadows and highlights in the same degree of intensity, for every figure.

Accessories

The painting of accessories may also be adapted to unify different figures which are put together. In our particular instance, the leather items, like the first figure's map case, and the second figure's pistol holster, are similarly painted, and the light effects are rendered approximately the same way. The basic colour for leather parts is Leather Brown 871, highlighted with Orange Brown 981 and shadowed with Black 950. I applied some weathering effects by selectively stroking the surface with pure Orange Brown, especially on the edges and rims.

The scenic base

The technique I use for leather items consists of applying different, very diluted, shades of brown, with a stabbing motion of the brush. This gives a realistic faded, degraded, used leather effect.

The setting of the figures is a vital element for the effectiveness and the credibility of the vignette. For this project, we looked for some kind of device that would locate the figures in a particular environment, but we did not want to have recourse to large size objects or buildings, because we felt this could detract from the main focus of the vignette, the figures themselves.

The figures are supposed to be in Italy, so we thought of a minimalist yet suggestive approach, consisting of showing the corner of a table, covered with a characteristic check tablecloth; and, as a fitting addition, a typical, traditional-style bottle of Chianti wine.

By the simple expedient of including these 'props', the image of an Italian *trattoria* can be conjured up. At the same time, the selection of these elements nicely adds to the celebration atmosphere, which we wanted to develop.

The table came from another kit. It was cut to the desired size, fitting it to the boundaries of the scenic base. The tablecloth was fashioned from very thinly rolled Milliput putty, cut to size and moulded over the table. The drapes were replicated by forming the proper shapes with round brush handles. The bottle was scratchbuilt from the same putty. A blob of it was put round a toothpick, which was then rotated, lathe-fashion, by hand, and the putty slowly shaped with moistened fingers. Once the basic shape was obtained, I let it cure and incorporated the details.

The various elements, attached to the base and painted. A typical check pattern was chosen for the tablecloth. The bottle was painted in dark green and varnished with gloss. The straw cover texture was imitated with thin vertical contrasting lines.

Colour Chart No.3: Luftwaffe splinter reversed colours

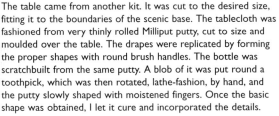

Base colour			
		Desert Yellow 977	Buff 976
	Mixing ratio:	50 per cent	50 per cent
Red Brown			
		Mahogany Brown 846	Desert Yellow 977
	Mixing ratio:	70 per cent	30 per cent
Medium Green			
		Olive Grey 888	Buff 976
	Mixing ratio	70 per cent	30 per cent

THIS PAGE Different views of the finished vignette. The table and bottle give depth to a scene, which, in itself, has a fairly flat composition. These elements, with their bright finishes, contribute a note of colour and balance to the otherwise predominating drab hues of the uniforms. The wooden floor was painted in dark tones, helping the figures to stand out.

'Tactical withdrawal': Fallschirmjäger on the Eastern Front, 1944

Subject:	Fallschirmjäger in winter uniforms
Project overview:	Building a diorama: design, storytelling and development. Figure superdetailing and conversion techniques. Tips for painting white uniforms.
Modellers:	Jaume Ortiz and Daniel Alfonsea
Skill level:	Master
Base kits:	DML Dragon no. 6157, 2nd Fallschirmjager Division (Kirovograd, Winter 1942/43); DML Dragon no. 6118 5cm Pak 38 w/ Fallschirmjägers
Scale:	1/35
Additional materials used:	Milliput Silver White two-part modelling putty, Tamiya: X-21 Flat Base, Tamiya Surface Primer no. 87026
Paints:	Matt Black 950, Brown Sand 876, Basic Skintone 815, Burnt Cadmium Red 814, Camo Pale Violet Brown 825, Chocolate Brown 872, German Orange 805, Flat Brown 984, Offwhite 820, Iraqi Sand 819, Royal Blue 809, German Luftwaffe Blue 816, Grey Green 866, Medium Grey 987, German Camouflage Black Brown 822, Buff 976

Introduction

As previously mentioned, Fallschirmjäger fought as elite infantry on the Eastern Front, where they followed the fortunes of the Wehrmacht. Paratrooper units were present in the Leningrad, Ukraine, Smolensk and Zhitomir campaigns, to name but a few.

For our final project, we decided to create a winter scene, in order to illustrate the cold weather uniforms. Fallschirmjäger did not have any specific winter gear – they were issued the same garments as the rest of the Luftwaffe units. For the time of our scene, this means the two-piece reversible winter overclothing. Initially, this was white, reversible to variable hues of *feldgrau*, mouse grey or *feldblau*; this non-white side would later be manufactured from various camouflage patterns. A variation of the earlier design, frequently seen in wartime images of Luftwaffe personnel, was of quilted construction, either of vertical or diagonal design.

This chapter covers the building of a diorama; this discipline is generally considered the most challenging enterprise in figure or AFV modelling, because of the increased difficulty of ensuring the balance and interaction between elements that usually call for figure conversion work. The painting techniques in this section will be focused on white clothing.

The diorama depicts a winter withdrawal scene, which is an image often associated with the Eastern Front, as it is of the more distant Napoleonic invasion. In fact, we believe our scene is strongly reminiscent of the 1812 campaign, with its horse-drawn gun!

A Jäger from 9. Jäger Regiment 43 in full winter uniform, Russia 1943. (From Osprey Publishing's Men-at-Arms 229: *Luftwaffe Field Divisions*.)

The idea is to suggest a *kampfgruppe*-style grouping, retreating to new positions after some Russian assault has broken through the former front line. The urgency of the situation is hinted at by the motley appearance of the group, and by the obviously improvised method of hauling an anti-tank gun by means of a commandeered horse.

We found an elongated, linear composition particularly well suited to the subject; and it looks like the elements included are but a small part of a larger column, which the viewer may imagine, beyond the edges of the diorama's base. The groundwork represents a mountain road – the sloping ground serves the purpose of avoiding level lines, parallel to the base, hence allowing for a more appealing composition. It also permits the incorporation of a rocky wall, which serves as a backdrop for the scene.

Composing a diorama requires the arrangement of numerous elements (scenery, figures, vehicles) and the creation of a scene that answers to your

OPPOSITE PAGE **The completed diorama 'Tactical withdrawal'.**

initial idea; at the same time it must be understandable and visually attractive to the viewer. Planning is fundamental, and sketches and mock-ups are very useful, although, more often than not, you will introduce changes along the way, either backtracking or exploring new paths. A diorama will be all the more effective if you manage to integrate these elements into successful storytelling, which will add a further dimension to the work.

Converting the figures

Figures in regular reversible uniforms are included in several Dragon offerings; I selected kit no. 6157. On the other hand, figures in quilted reversible uniforms are available only as crew inside various gun kits, like nos. 6056 and 6118.

Dragon figure sets are not designed as multiposable; some degree of limb interchange is feasible, but you must check the coherence and continuity of the various parts, to ensure they really match, to avoid unnatural or strange poses. Of course, if you are ready to do some reworking/remodelling, then the scope widens a lot. This has an added advantage: although Dragon figures are generally correct in terms of pose, many of them are uninteresting or dull, while not completely stiff, so playing around with the different limbs and remodelling them when needed will result in more satisfactory figures; this is a skill that pays dividends when you design figures to fit a particular action, for vignettes or dioramas.

Take as an example the first figure, clad in the regular two-part reversible uniform, which comprises parts from several figures in kit no. 6157: body C, left leg C, right leg B, and left arm A. A Hornet head with a winter cap completed the ensemble. The right arm was scratchbuilt. I armed him with a captured PpSh 41 sub machine gun, a weapon appreciated for its large capacity magazine.

The second figure wears the padded two-part uniform. I used all four major components of a gunner from kit no. 6056, in a kneeling stance, plus a Hornet paratrooper head. The third figure wears a mismatched uniform, padded jacket and regular trousers; consequently, the legs came from kit no. 6157 again (right D and left A), the body and arms from a couple of the crewmen in kit no. 6118. The head is an Alpine Miniatures spare.

Regarding individual equipment, Dragon does not score highly. Some of it is not adequately detailed; worse still, a good number of items are consistently too small. So, you either have to rework the detail or substitute some of the pieces with better offerings from other sources, or scratchbuild them.

An important consideration often overlooked is that of equipment placing and hanging. In the real world, these items are attached by straps, hooks, rings or other devices, from where they may hang at a certain specific angle; they react to gravity and to the wearer's movements, and adapt to his body. Frequently, just attaching the part in place with a drop of glue will not be enough. So, you have to check if the scale items you are using have these details correct; if not, you must modify or add them, and you must further ensure that the ensemble looks both accurate and realistic.

For variety, I thought it would be a good idea to include a Medical Specialist, from a Medical Battalion attached to a Fallschirmjäger Division. These troops could be found in a field hospital, for instance, not in the frontline; and general issue field-blue Luftwaffe uniforms would be more prevalent. Their *waffenfarbe* would be the medical troops' dark 'cornflower' blue; on the other hand, a company medic would be very much clad like his comrades.

So, the figure wears a field-blue greatcoat (collar patches had been discontinued since 1942), with cornflower-blue *waffenfarbe* on his shoulder straps, and the medical Asclepius badge on his left sleeve. The helmet is a conventional M35, usually worn without decals at this date. He has been lucky enough to acquire a pair of felt and leather winter boots, of which several models existed.

Also, our specialist carries specific medical equipment: on his belt, a pair of 'dismounted medical pouches'; and the M1939 medical pack on his back, which was a version of the general issue pack.

I combined various Dragon parts in order to find an appropriate basic pose. These are provisionally put together with Blu-Tack, so I can play around with them and see the effect.

This is a more definitive mock-up. I decided to scratchbuild the right arm, having no suitable stock part.

The resulting piece, ready to be primed. A Hornet head is always a good improvement to add.

Swapping parts between figures frequently entails reworking the area of insertion of arms to trunk, and of legs to trunk and between the legs themselves, to fit the new poses, both with regard to anatomy and to the crease pattern.

A close-up of the equipment. Here I used Andrea Miniatures' water bottle and cooking pot. The breadbag is scratchbuilt; the pistol holster is a modified Dragon item, to which I added some bulk.

This figure was converted from a couple of kneeling artillerymen. The crotch area, legs and right arm received the most work. You can see the wire insertions at the knee joints.

This was the most detailed conversion in the whole diorama, because of the very specific stance we wanted to represent: we intended to portray a soldier pushing the anti-tank gun through the muddy ground, as if to help the horse drag it past a difficult stretch. This meant the figure had to be carefully adapted to the gun's shield and the terrain, and, not surprisingly, no out-of-the box figure was suitable. So, I selected a couple of legs from the spares box, and further converted them by means of reworking some of the articulations, at pelvis, waist, knee or ankle level. Winter boots were more voluminous than those on the standard model, so I substituted a pair of Airfix 1/32-scale boots for the original 1/35 footwear, to provide some more bulk. A greatcoat-clad

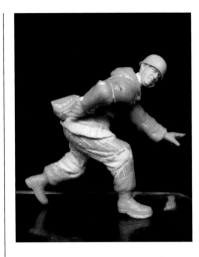

A more advanced stage. The left arm is still not fixed – it had to be in contact with the anti-tank gun's wheel, so needed to be carefully adapted to the wheel's position.

On the reworked joints, I had to reconstruct the quilted pattern too, trying to keep it in harmony with the original design. The major changes in the pelvis area called for a new jacket skirt.

The definitive pose. The insertion area of the right arm had to be rebuilt in answer to the new pose. MP40 ammunition triple pocket pouches were cut down to their individual components and assembled again, adapted to the body.

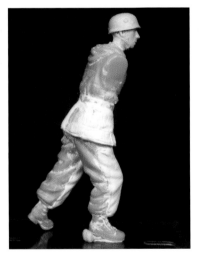

Equipment details. Note how all of the attachment devices have been reproduced and respond to the body shape and movement. This is frequently overlooked, but in real life these items are not just glued in place, nor are they impervious to gravity.

This one is a composite figure, comprising parts from several figures in two different Dragon boxes, to obtain a forward-leaning walking pose. The trouser legs and pelvis, again, needed some surface reworking to match the new needs.

At this stage, the arm poses had not been fully established – these had to be defined in conjunction with the development of the horse, to which this soldier is to be closely related.

torso was drawn from Dragon's kit no. 6190, making sure the spine curve was appropriate for our purposes, to which a pair of arms from Dragon's kit no. 6158 was adapted, and hands substituted with more suitable alternatives. I used a helmeted Warriors' head to top it all.

The felt-and-leather composition of the boots was reproduced over the regular jackboot. The legs themselves did not require much surface remodelling, just at the left knee area, because they would be largely covered by the greatcoat's skirt.

The definitive stance. Note the leaning of the figure is more pronounced now. I found I had to increase the effect, when matching the figure to the ground it was to be inserted in, for the pose to work.

I used a Dragon folding entrenching tool, on which I replaced the handle with a more substantial one, and added some details. Partly visible is the FG42 ammunition bandoleer. This did not dangle freely from the neck, being attached to the belt.

An initial mock-up. I selected parts from several figures, and almost every joint had to be modified. I modelled a pair of winter felt-and-leather boots. These were fairly bulky, so I used 1/32-scale boots which I built up further.

As you can see, this figure was mostly scratchbuilt, its various components being just a foundation for putty. I needed a particular pose, for a very concrete action: usually, this means some major reworking.

The pose was deliberately designed to be off balance. This results in a more appealing stance. Pay attention to the shoulder area: a pose like this creates bunched-up clothing between the blades.

A detail of the breadbag. Scratchbuilding these pieces has the added advantage that you can adapt them to the surface of the body. I modelled it suspended from its cross strap, for variety, instead of the more usual placement at the belt. Note also the backpack straps, finished off with a Historex buckle.

The skirt itself was made with thinly rolled Milliput, cut to the approximate shape and applied in place after a few minutes, to allow for a little curing, which facilitates manipulation; this is best done in two sessions, beginning with the right half and, when fully cured, next adding the left half, which overlaps it. Putty does not behave like real cloth in scale, so we have to help gravity with some judicious tool intervention. In this way, basic draping effects will be accomplished. Once dry, we have to add more putty, and enhance the

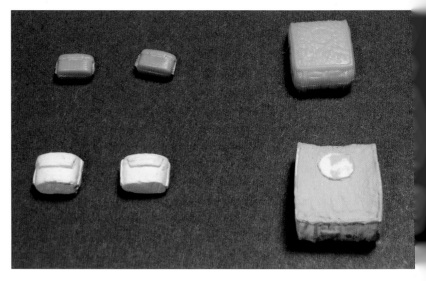

Dragon's breadbags are consistently undersize; discarding them is advisable, substituting them with better alternatives; alternatively you can make them from scratch, as I did. In this case, the buttoned tabs are hanging free, because this bag would be suspended from a strap, and not attached to the belt.

Medical equipment, like these twin belt pouches and backpack, can be found in some Dragon boxes, but again, reference to sources proves them to be too small, so I built these examples anew. The difference is certainly noticeable, justifying the work.

shape with more folds and wrinkles. The last part will be applying such details as pocket flaps, rear opening panels and the like.

The original torso was reworked at the arm insertion areas, because of the specific posture, which causes some bunching up. Shoulder straps were rebuilt in kind. The original arms' surface detail would be removed and completely remodelled to match the new stance.

As far as equipment is concerned, we checked Dragon's medical equipment, such as that found in kit no. 6074, against several references, and found it wanting in size, it being way too small; hence, both pouches and knapsack were scratchbuilt. The breadbag was built anew too, and shown hanging from its cloth strap, instead of from the belt, for variety. Appropriate straps for it and the knapsack were modelled on the body.

The horse

The noble beast in our scene began life as one of the pair in Esci's Supply Wagon set. Its pose and expression were not suitable for my aims: this horse would be walking up a muddy mountain road, pulling an anti-tank gun, so its body language had to adapt both to the terrain and to the effort that the action implies. Besides this, the neutral expression on its face had to be transformed into a more suggestive one. Last but not least, I thought it would be interesting to portray a heavier draft horse, hence some more conversion work would be in order.

I began by sawing through the majority of the horse's joints, and reassembling the legs in the desired pose; this was done on an inclined base, with a degree of inclination similar to the one in the scene. The leaning forward of the horse was deliberately forced, to convey the idea of its struggling uphill. The head was placed on a length of wire, over which the new neck would be built. The head and neck were placed at angles appropriate to the body language.

I studied the characteristics of the major breeds of draft horses, but instead of portraying a particular one, made a hybrid of the most common ones, so obtaining a readily recognizable (and credible) work animal: a heavily built, stocky horse, with powerful neck and a substantial head, and typical details like hairy fetlocks and docked tail. Hence, the horse was remodelled with this image in mind.

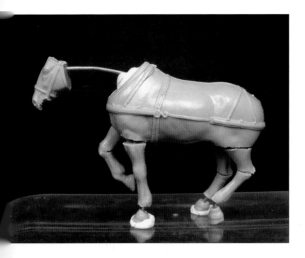

An initial mock-up. The original horse had a placid walking stance that did not suit the setting. I sawed almost every one of its leg joints, and assembled the parts with wire lengths, to create the new pose. The neck part had a pose too different to the one I had in mind, so I just discarded it and joined the head to the body with wire.

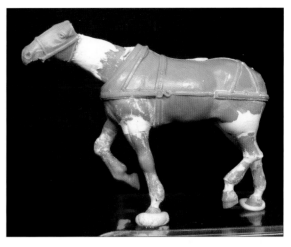

The pose is almost fixed by now, and the joints have been set. A foundation for the neck has been modelled. I removed the lower jaw, because I wanted to model an open mouth.

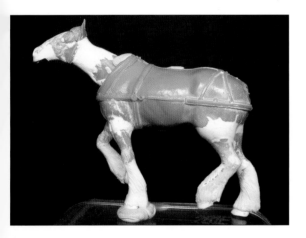

The legs' muscular volume has been built up. The upper legs did not need to be detailed much, because this area would eventually be mostly hidden from view. The lower legs required more work. I also added hairy fetlocks. The hooves needed some volume and detailing. Remodelling of the head has begun, including facial features, like the eyes.

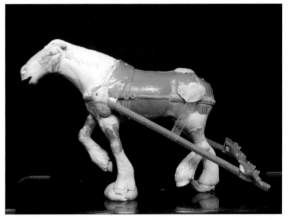

The neck is more or less finished, the mane is just an initial shape. The head is very much defined at this stage. Note the flared nostrils, outstretched muzzle, and thrown back ears. The head straps have been carved down, to be rebuilt later in a new configuration. You can see I have begun to work on the gun assembly, here propped on the horse.

The horse's facial features were also tackled, and modified to show ears thrown back, flared nostrils, and front teeth showing through the tense muzzle – all increasing the impression of a jittery and toiling animal.

As a final touch, I gave the horse some snow camouflage, in the form of an improvised cover made of nondescript cloth, like bedding. This was again made with Milliput, rolled very thin. The use of such covers is confirmed by contemporary sources. Finally, to go over this, I designed a harness to pull the gun: it consists of a makeshift concoction, the bare minimum to serve its function, something that soldiers could have jury-rigged from assorted materials at hand combined with a farm harness.

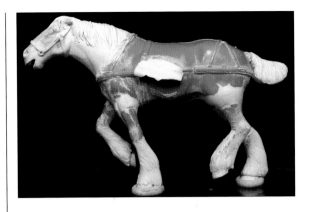

ABOVE The horse is basically finished. Note that the head, in the end, was almost completely rebuilt, the original one having been used just as a foundation. The upper teeth are visible in the mouth. The mane has been finished too. The halter type bridle is now nearly complete. I chose to model a docked tail.

ABOVE RIGHT A closer view. The halter straps were modelled appropriately to the action: so, they are close to the left cheek, but separate from the right, in response to the pulling of the reins in this direction. The reins would be attached later on, in close relationship with the horse handler's pose.

RIGHT The lower straps have been added to the halter. For the horse covering it was important to suggest a flowing effect. I made it with very thinly rolled Milliput. Some damage was incorporated at the lower edges, for a frayed appearance.

Painting winter camouflage uniforms

In this chapter painting techniques will be dealt with in a more general form, focusing on the painting of white camouflage garments, these being the most conspicuous in the diorama.

When painting winter camouflage, we must have in mind that, because of the scale effect, absolute white must be avoided. The amount of light a miniature figure reflects has to be proportional to its size, that is, it will reflect less light than the real thing. Therefore, we should restrict the use of pure white, because in this way we can better play with contrast and will obtain a more realistic look.

I usually start with yellowish hues when painting white camouflage uniforms. If we look at contemporary photographs, we will notice that white garments easily lean to yellowish or brownish hues, and weathering and soiling effects run the whole gamut from buff to dark brown.

Even if I choose several tones to paint the different whites in the figures' uniforms, I try to keep a degree of coherence between them, for the diorama to look like a unified whole.

The first figure is clad completely in white. The basic colour for the jacket is a mix of Offwhite 820 with Buff 976, in a 50:50 ratio. For the trousers, instead of Buff, I used Iraqi Sand 819, in the same proportion. I executed the shadowing

This view shows the frontal, overlapping opening to advantage. A couple of fastening straps would be added later on. I decided to keep the existing body harness, which I would modify to fit my purposes.

A rear view. Note how thin Milliput putty can be rolled. Plenty of talcum powder is needed for this task. The covering is meant to be made of thin cloth, like bedding sheets or a tablecloth; I tried to suggest this by means of the wrinkle pattern and the flowing of the skirts.

effects with the same colour, Chocolate Brown 872, added to the basic mix for both. I try to keep the highlights under control, to avoid too white a final look; only the uppermost highlights are rendered with straight Offwhite.

The second figure wears white again, this time a quilted uniform. I made use of the same mixes, but this time with German Camouflage Black Brown 822, instead of Chocolate Brown, added for the shadows. This results in a fairly greyish tone, which gives a 'colder' aspect to the figure, but within the same general range of colour.

I tackled the quilted pattern by painting the dividing lines to define the squares, and next highlighting and shadowing every one of these squares individually, thus conferring volume on them. This is a slow and tedious process, but the final results are well worth the effort.

The third figure, on the other hand, wears just his trousers white-side out. These were painted with Offwhite 820 mixed with Medium Grey 987 as a base colour. This is a greyish, colder mix compared to the previously described 'whites'. Shadowing, again, was made with the addition of German Camouflage Black Brown.

This figure's jacket shows its grey side, which I reproduced with Grey Green 866, highlighted with Basic Skintone 815, and shadowed with Black 950. I enhanced the volume of the quilted pattern, dealing separately with the light effects of every single square.

The fourth figure is the only one not clad in white garments. His overcoat and trousers share the same basic mix, German Luftwaffe Blue 816 highlighted with Basic Skintone 815, and shadowed with a mixture of Royal Blue 809 plus Black 950. This I did because I found that mixing just Black resulted in too greyish a hue, and the characteristic blue-grey tone of Luftwaffe uniforms became lost.

The first figure. I reproduced the effects of mud splotches and soiling by 'stabbing' the wet surface with various brown shades.

Seams can be successfully rendered by painting a dark-coloured line immediately besides a light one. This same technique is used, in a *trompe l'oeil* effect, to reproduce those seams that are not actually modelled.

Some Luftwaffe equipment was manufactured in *feldblau* canvas, for instance, bread bags, like this one, which I painted in German Luftwaffe Blue 816. I imitated a faded and chipped white camouflaged cooking pot, applying very thin white washes to the basic dark-green surface.

The second figure, finished. For the weathering, I selected shades that made a good combination with the white uniform.

Again, aluminium accessories were painted first in Black Green 980, and next a worn effect was suggested with an application, on specific points, of Offwhite 820 mixed with Oily Steel 865.

The helmet was painted in colours similar to those of the uniform, and I selected some grey and brown tones, which I used in very thinned form for the weathering.

Another view of the completed second figure.

The third figure. Canvas ammunition bandoliers were made in several colours. The most commonly seen type for the FG42 magazines was in 'splinter' camouflage, the same as for the uniforms already mentioned.

The FG42 rifle sling is fastened with two tiny photoetch carbine hooks. Note the different materials for the butt (plastic) and the forestock (wood).

Take your time when painting the numerous accoutrements; this will pay dividends, providing attention-drawing details.

I painted the horse's sheet with the same basic colour as mentioned for the first and second figures, that is, Offwhite 820 with Iraqi Sand 819, plus German Camouflage Black Brown 822 for the shadows. The animal itself I painted as a dark bay, with a base of Flat Brown 984, highlighted with German Orange 805 and shadowed with Black. I laid down these lighting effects by means of short brush strokes, following the growth direction of the hair; this makes for a good representation of the surface of the skin.

I also consulted appropriate references and added a selection of details to the horse, such as face markings and leg stockings, which were faithfully imitated; incorporating such eye-catching details to a model horse does make a difference, giving much more realism to the subject.

An important factor common to every one of the figures in the scene is the weathering, which in this particular case is heavy because of the wet and muddy conditions. This gives further visual unification to the separate components, and anchors them to the groundwork, by physically incorporating the terrain onto the figures. The effects were concentrated on the lower parts of their bodies: boots, trousers, coat skirts, etc.

It is pertinent to mention now that we consciously decided to keep these soiling effects quite contained. We made what we believe is a legitimate appeal to artistic licence. In real life, the figures would surely be abundantly covered with muck; but sticking to realism in this respect would be detrimental to the aesthetic qualities of the work, besides obliterating much detail, so we chose to tone the weathering down to an acceptable degree.

The thickest, wet, slush was fashioned with marble powder mixed with dark brown paint and gloss varnish, a paste of which was applied to the relevant

The fourth figure completed.

The felt part of the winter boots was textured by 'stabbing' the Brown Sand 876 mixed with Chocolate Brown 872 base colour with straight Brown Sand 876.

The helmet is painted with the same techniques as previously described, but this time in several shades of blue.

A rear view of the fourth figure.

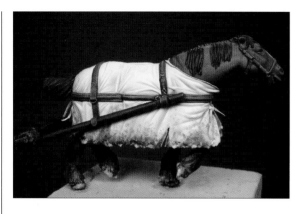
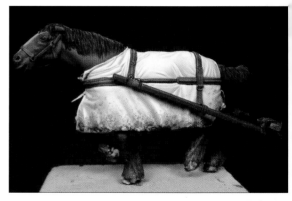

ABOVE Views of the completed horse. The harness is painted as leather, replicating seams and overlapping pieces with bold applications of light and shadow effects.

areas. Some touches of gloss varnish will later enhance the wet look where the mud is supposed to be fresher.

Dryer mud, being less voluminous, was treated differently. I wetted the receiving area with water, and next I applied small dots of Chocolate Brown 872 and Camo Pale Violet Brown 825 onto the moist surface. This allows for the merging of the paint on the basic uniform colour, and looks more realistic.

The groundwork

The terrain is modelled on a piece of styrofoam, cut at a vertical angle to simulate a sloped mountain track; this angle effectively contributes to the drama of the scene.

The rocks are pieces of cork bark, selected for their appropriate shape. The muddy track consists of synthetic foam, artificial grass, small bits of branches and white glue. I covered the entire surface with the resulting paste, and once it began to cure, I sculpted the furrows and the depressions representing pools.

I painted it in dark brown, with some orange brown in the deepest areas to suggest dirty water; finally, three or four layers of ceramic varnish were laid down, to achieve a wet look. The pools received a couple more layers, to confer some depth to the water.

I tried to represent two kinds of snow: the 'older' snow, half melted and half frozen, which covered the road and turned to mud; and the recently fallen snow, with a spongy and immaculate look.

The old snow is a mix of marble powder and gloss varnish, applied in a paste form. Once dry, it was weathered with various brown tones, and finally it received a coat of ceramic varnish.

The fresh snow was mixed with marble powder, Andrea Miniatures' artificial snow and white glue. This was laid on the rocks and the road margins. Andrea's product is the component that brings out the shiny reflections; hence, by varying the amount of it in the mix, a more or less glossy finish is achieved.

The base was cut from a piece of styrofoam.

The cork crust pieces, simulating rocks, and the paste imitating mud, have been already applied.

It is advisable to try the mud paste out on a small area before putting it on the entire surface, to be sure you are obtaining the desired effect.

Laying down the snow.

The finished groundwork, with the anti-tank gun in place.

RIGHT **The DML anti-tank gun superbly painted in a faded whitewash camouflage by our friend José Antonio Azorín.**

BELOW AND P.P.73–77 **Views of the completed diorama.**

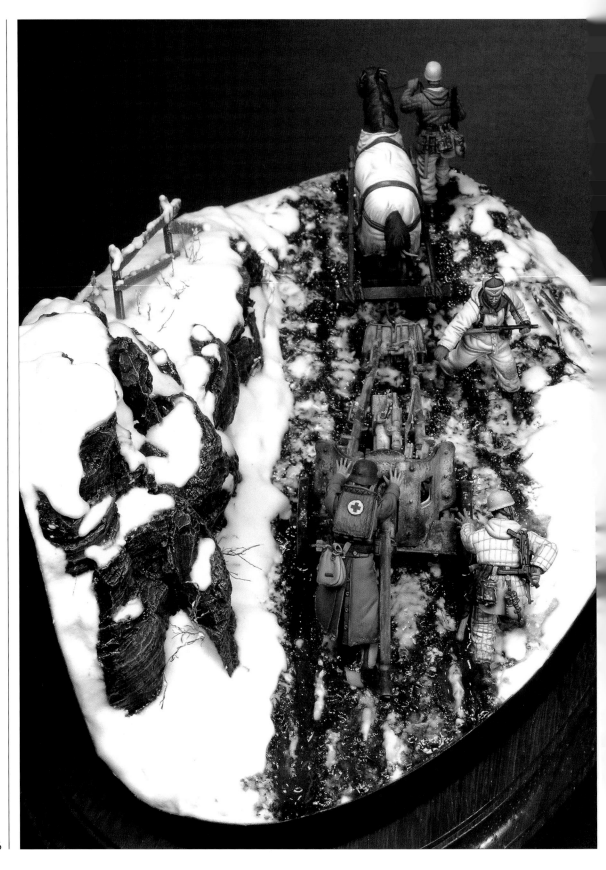

Bibliography and further reading

Ailsby, Christopher *Hitler's Sky Warriors*, Spellmount Limited, 2000.

Angolia, John R. *For Führer and Fatherland: Military Awards of the Third Reich*, Bender Publishing, 1987 (revised edition).

Angolia, John R. and Schlicht, Adolf *Uniforms and Traditions of the German Army 1933–45* (vol. 3), Bender Publishing, 1987.

Angolia, John R. and Schlicht, Adolf *Uniforms and Traditions of the Luftwaffe*, Bender Publishing, 1996 (vol. 1), 1997 (vol. 2), 1998 (vol. 3).

Antill, Peter *Crete 1941* (Campaign series no. 147), Osprey Publishing, 2005.

Baxter, I.M. and Volstad, Ronald *Fallschirmjäger*, Concord Publications, 2001.

Davis, Brian L. *Uniforms and Insignia of the Luftwaffe*, Arms and Armour Press, 1991 (vol. 1), 1995 (vol. 2).

Ellis, John *Cassino: The Hollow Victory*, Guild Publishing, 1985.

Ford, Ken *Cassino: The Four Battles*, Crowood Press, 2001.

Halcomb, Jill and Saris, Wilhelm P.B.R. *Headgear of Hitler's Germany* (vol. 1), Bender Publishing, 1989.

Kurtz, Robert *German Paratroops*, Schiffer Publishing, 2000.

Kurtz, Robert *Afrikakorps*, Schiffer Publishing, 2004.

Lucas, James *Storming Eagles*, Guild Publishing, 1988.

Mason, Chris *Fallschirmjäger* (Soldat series no. 8), Pictorial Histories Publishing, 2000.

Nasse, Jean-Yves *Green Devils*, Histoire & Collections, 1997.

Palinckx, Werner *Camouflage Uniforms of the German Wehrmacht*, Schiffer Publishing, 2002.

Quarrie, Bruce *German Airborne Troops* (Men-at-Arms series no. 139), Osprey Publishing, 1983.

Quarrie, Bruce *Fallschirmjäger* (Warrior series no. 38), Osprey Publishing, 2001.

Quarrie, Bruce *German Airborne Divisions: Blitzkrieg 1940–41* (Battle Orders series no. 4), Osprey Publishing, 2003.

Quarrie, Bruce *German Airborne Divisions: Mediterranean Theatre 1942–45* (Battle Orders series no. 15), Osprey Publishing, 2005.

Queen, Eric *Red Shines the Sun: a Pictorial History of the Fallschirm-Infanterie*, Bender Publishing, 2002.

Rottman, Gordon and Volstad, Ron *German Combat Equipments 1939–45* (Men-at-Arms series no. 234), Osprey Publishing, 1991.

Scipion, Jacques and Bastien, Yves *Afrikakorps*, Histoire & Collections, 1996.

Williamson, Gordon *World War II German Battle Insignia* (Men-at-Arms series no. 365), Osprey Publishing, 2002.

Osprey Publishing's Men-at-Arms 139: *German Airborne Troops*.

Recommended websites

Green Devils   www.greendevils.com/greendevils

Fallschirmjäger 1936–45   www.eagle19.freeserve.co.uk/index.html

15 Kp. Fsch. Jg. Regt. 5   www.fjr5.com

Wehrmacht Awards   www.wehrmacht-awards.com

Feldgrau   www.feldgrau.com/index.html

Figures available

Alpine Miniatures	
35020	German paratrooper with PzSchreck
35021	German paratrooper

Andrea Miniatures	
S5-F13	German Fallschirmjäger sniper, 1941
S5-F20	German Fallschirmjäger, 1943
S5-F29	German Fallschirmjäger, Ardennes 1944
S5-F33	German paratrooper, Italy 1943
S5-F36	German paratrooper major, 1944
S5-F47	German Fallschirmjäger, 1941

Dragon	
1617	Fallschirmjäger (Gran Sasso rescue 1943) (1/16)
1628	Fallschirmjäger Batallion 500 (1/16)
6077	German Fallschirmjäger with donkeys
6094	Gran Sasso Raid (Otto Skorzeny & Fallschirmjäger)
6113	1/35 3rd Fallschirmjäger Division (Ardennes 1944)
6143	1/35 3rd Fallschirmijäger Division (Ardennes 1944) Part 2
6145	1/35 SS-Fallschirmjäger Batallion 500 (Drvar, 1944)
6157	2nd Fallschirmjäger Division (Kirovograd, winter 1942/43)
6195	Fallschirmjäger Regiment 3 (Sicily 1943)
6215	1/35 Fallschirmjäger 8cm mortar team (Italy 1944)
6276	1st Fallschirmjager Division Holland 1940 – Gen2

Hornet	
GH 24	German Luftwaffe paratrooper
HGH 06 5	Heads, German WWII paratrooper helmet

Jaguar	
JA61603	German paratrooper, 1943 (120mm)
JA61611	Oberleutnant, 2nd Paratrooper Assault Division (120mm)
JA63009	German paratrooper at rest (2)
JA63010	German paratrooper 'Got a light?' (2)
JA63601	'Was in himmel?!'

Legend	
CE-0015	German paratrooper, standing
CE-0032	German paratrooper W/MG-34, Normandy
CE-0033	German paratroopers, WWII (2 figures)
CE-0058	German paratrooper, Ukraine, winter 1943
CE-0069	German Fallschirmjäger, wearing camo

Verlinden Productions	
1255	1:35 Fallschirmjägers
1766	1:35 Fallschirmjäger assault
1767	1:35 Fallschirmjäger MG team
1812	1:35 German paratrooper gun/mortar crew (3 figures)
1860	1:35 German paratrooper MG team
2011	1:35 Game Over German paratroopers WWII
1210	120mm German paratrooper
1228	120mm German paratrooper/jump suit

Warriors	
WA 16037	German Fallschirmjäger throwing Stick grenade (120 mm)
WA 35055	German Heads 4: Fallschirmjäger
WA 35118	Fallschirmjäger helmets
WA 35410	Fallschirmjaeger (Semovente-SPG) crew
WA 35418	Fallschirmjaeger mortar team (4 figures in camouflage)
WA 35439	Fallschirmjäger, advancing with rifle at ready
WA 35444	Wounded Fallschirmjäger
WA 35459	Fallschirmjäger running, firing MP 40

Wolf	
WAW 18	German paratrooper with ammo
WSH 03	German paratrooper
WSH 11	German paratrooper
WSH 18	German paratrooper with barrow
WSH 39	German paratrooper carrying firewood

Index